T[...]

of

MOTHER AFRICA

THE CRY

of

MOTHER AFRICA

CHARLES KAPUNGWE

Foreword by
His Excellency the President
Dr. Kenneth David Kaunda

"What an accomplishment and masterpiece!!"
– Rev. John Preacher
– Former English Professor at Allen University,
South Carolina U.S.A.

CK

Second edition printed by Charles Kapungwe 2020
published by:
CharlieKaps®
Columbia, SC 29204 U.S.A.

First published 2015
ISBN: 978-0-9986663-6-5 Print – Paperback
Library of Congress Control Number: 2020920017

Acknowledgments

I would like to thank the first President of the Republic of Zambia, His Excellency Dr. Kenneth David Kaunda, he accepted to write the foreword to this book and found time in spite of his busy schedule. I would like to thank the Rev. John Preacher, my Professor of English at Allen University, Columbia, South Carolina for inspiring me to write this work, and for important corrections. I also would love to thank Rev. Leroy Cannon and his wife Helen, my parents in U.S.A., without whom this work could not have materialised. My gratitude also goes to Dr. Charles E. Young, President of Allen University, Bishop Robert Webster, Rev. Dr. Paul Bupe and his wife Catherine; Bishop Elijah Mboho and his wife Princess, Rev. Sunday Etim and his wife Rev. Imaikop, and the Goodnews Community Church International in Columbia, South Carolina. Others whom I would like to acknowledge are Mr. Robert Rabias and his wife Mrs. Joellyn Rabias, Mr. Steve Marbert and his wife Kathy and New Covenant Presbyterian Church, Aiken, South Carolina. I am also thankful to my father and mother, Mr. Amos Kapungwe and Nancy Kapungwe and last but not least, Trinity A.M.E. Church, Jordan Chapel A.M.E. Church and Calvary Temple A.M.E. Church in Kitwe, Zambia. Special thanks to Rev. Aaron Siwale and wife, Rev. Richard Kasanda and wife Pamela and Br. Christopher Chikulungu and wife and Br. Joseph Siwo and his wife.

PREFACE

When I arrived in the U.S.A. for the second time in 2000, I refused to be drawn into any racial disputes. My first visit had been seven years earlier. Coming from Zambia, a country in which racism is almost non-existent or at least uncommon or not an issue at all, I declared my stand immediately, to be an ambassador of my culture. This book, therefore, is not a tool for any racial attack on any group or groups of people but a voice against tyrants in white collars who look innocent but are responsible for half of the world's misery and turmoil today.

My calling and work as a minister, also demanded that I transcended above a party spirit. My terms of reference were, therefore, very clear. I was not to be drawn into any anger, bitterness, vengeance, and hatred which but are all results of such conflicts of racism and segregation. From the outset, my mission was declared. It was that of reconciliatory and not that of a divider. It was also going to be that of the healer and not that meant to injure. I endeavoured to stand to that cause. Nevertheless, living between the two worlds soon produced deep and great insights. These insights, unfortunately, raised a lot of questions, and consequently, demanded a lot of answers too. They were questions that every African asks daily. Perhaps some scholars and political pundits who lived before me had already given answers to these nagging questions.

My explorative mind, however, refused to relent and settle. It implored me to pen the anguish of many an African child. It is my prayer that the objective of this writing be met, that objective is to find solutions to Africa's problems and difficulties that she has encountered for centuries. It is also my prayer that instead of vengeance there may be forgiveness, instead of hatred, love and instead of bitterness joy. My objectives would not be met also if on the other hand "Africa's enemies" refuse to budge and continue to exploit the "weak." May the Lord guide you as you begin to read this book and may you contribute to the healing of all mankind that justice may prevail instead of exploitation, manipulation, and theft. May God bless you all.

Charles Kapungwe
Columbia, South Carolina U.S.A.
January 15, 2015.

Foreword by His Excellency the President Dr. Kenneth David Kaunda

Charles Kapungwe's book, *Cry of Mother Africa*, is not only a lament about Africa's situation over a long period, but a call to act with the courage we have within us and to improve things in this, our one world.

The poetry collection is both a cry and a fight. Having been a health worker, Christian Reverend, and writer, amongst other things, Charles Kapungwe's writing, with deep passion, draws upon issues from various areas of human endeavour. He uses well his experience of living in Africa and outside the continent.

As Charles celebrates the well-endowed beauty and resources of Africa and her people, he laments on the long exploitation and suppression of Africa's people by fellow human beings. Over the centuries, on the continent and in the diaspora where persons of Africa descent are living, we have come from the traumatic situations of slave trade, colonialism, racism, and apartheid forced upon us.

Exploitation, suppression, and humiliation is what many of us fought against when we were fighting for independence and even after we got into government. As we begin the Twenty-First Century, the situation of injustice in terms of Africa's people and resources is still there. It is heartening when Charles Kapungwe urges Africa's people to rise and take control of their journey. For long term prosperity, it is important to cooperate and harness our resources under an Africa united across people and borders.

Like other fellow brothers and sisters all over the world, Africa and her people must be treated with respect and dignity. In the poetry in *Cry of Mother Africa*, frank Charles Kapungwe openly and fearlessly brings out discussion around human relations involving Africa and the world. The message is strong and relevant to our times.

Charles Kapungwe's writing succeeds both as message and well written song. Readers will have various views about Charles Kapungwe's writing. Important is that the poet has brought us urgent messages to think about and consider where Africa and the whole world have been and should be. There should be healing of relationships in this, our one world. We need fair play in all areas. It is my hope that men, women, and young persons from various backgrounds will do much to help realise this vision.

Reverend Charles Kapungwe's message reaches us with an urgency calling for our immediate action. May the reader of *Cry of Mother Africa* be awakened to action for the common good of humanity!

Kenneth D Kaunda,
First President of the Republic of Zambia, LUSAKA.
6th June, 2014.

CONTENTS

THE CRY OF MOTHER AFRICA

CHAPTER 1

MOTHER AFRICA: AMAZINGLY ENDOWED WITH BEAUTY AND RICHES!

Africa, Mother Africa!
Land of virgin natural resources.
From the Alps (Atlas Mountains) of north Morocco
To Drakensberg Mountains of South Africa,
Your undulating landscape takes a deep breath-taking sigh;
It speaks of your awesome scenery.
From the summit of Mt. Kilimanjaro in East Africa,
To Guinea Bissau's mangroves of West Africa –
You are a product of a Great Landscaper!
Showered and blessed with the ancient Nile,
The mighty Congo, the imposing Niger, the great
        Zambezi Rivers,
Phenomenon you are!

Great scenarios endow you.
Roaming elephants, rhinoceros,
the lion: King of the African jungle, the leopard,
Buffalo – all in their natural habitations,
with singing birds overshadowing you, a beautiful sight!
Home to the baobab tree, the palm tree,
the cocoa tree,

and the savannah camouflaging your animals from
      ferocious beasts!
Blessed with the Great Lakes,
gigantic Rift Valley of East Africa,
the gorgeous Victoria Falls – a wonder of wonders you are!
A masterpiece of a great handmanship.

Oh, give me your palm oil, Mother Africa!
That I may rub my dry-bruised skin.
Your lotion may soothe my scars,
Incurred by vehicles of oppression and injustice.
Give me your gold, diamond, silver, copper, uranium,
      emerald,
And withhold not your crude oil.
O Mother of great riches!
Product of your sweat enriches another man!
You watch while they reap open your ground –
A fountain of wealth!
Who told you, you were a continent of poverty?
Who told you to believe in a lie?
O poor land!

Your laps and breasts have nursed dignitaries.
Your breasts now hang limp and dry,
A laughingstock of your adversaries,
who stripped you naked and partitioned you!

Your sweat is an odour of production of wealth.
No sooner you melt your labour
than your perspiration becomes a stench to his nostrils.
Oh, Mother of civilisation!
Who cast lots against you, –

so that now the river separates your family, your clan?
Your watershed divides friendship.
Your valley swallows up relations.
Now your neighbour is your enemy!
You are now a colony of Who? What?
You are Francophone! Anglophone! Lusophone!
An embittered seed of animosity is sown among your
    brothers.
Who shall remove the weed?

You have enriched your master, Oh Africa!
Your sweat subsidizes another man's house.
You continue to wallow in poverty in the midst of
    riches!
Now he pours scorn on your nakedness.
He parades your shame on a box.
It ought not to be, oh mother of wealth!

Awake from slumber and get wisdom.
Lay down your arms.
Think O ye adversaries!
Loose off your shackles of imperialism.
For great is your future,
and mighty are your sons and daughters.
Let the nozzle be directed at Africa.
Do not render help to those who siphon off your wealth.
And be proud of your rich heritage.

Your morning sun is a ray of hope
That radiates rays of love
Shining on your waters,
Upon her expanse with superb beauty

3

The Divine's remembrance of you.
His presence, an aroma of His Majestic glory,
And the sunset your marvellous glory.
A reflection of your meekness,
which someone exploited as your weakness,
But as a charming mother,
You continue to give out your love, O Africa!

You stand out among your nobles
As a peculiar people,
who opens her doors to a stranger
Giving bread to her enemies,
And sanctuary to perpetrators of oppression and
        injustice.
Your weakness is your strength
That overcomes victimization and stigmatisation.
Your toil, an endless painful yoke you bear.

Your fallen heroes propounded unity.
They treasured love, hard work, and communal living!
Kwame Nkrumah, Augustino Neto,
Sir Seretse Khama, Jomo Kenyatta,
Anwar Sadat, Mwarimu Julius Nyerere
William Tobert, Samora Machel, –
Symbols of your unfailing love
That defies understanding.

Your traditions are a spring of knowledge
Speaking of your rich culture,
Passed on from your ancestors,
Who marvel at your now lost identity and dignity,
As you fell into your enemy's trap,

And the arrows and spears of bitterness
pierced your gorgeous brown flesh,
Oozing drops of blood that speak of love
And cry for justice and equal opportunity!

Why do you let your customer determine the price?
Why do you let him plunder your wealth?
He steals from you in broad daylight!
Awake and learn a lesson from a chicken,
O mother of abundance!
And protect all your offspring under your wings.

Your enemies reap where they did not sow,
They gather from another man's field,
Collecting what is not rightfully theirs
Into their barns, the harvest they put
Leftovers, they leave
Crumbs for my mother and her children to pick up,
Unmindful, too, that on their little fingers they step,
As the helpless family tries to pick up,
leftovers that they may live
Like a partridge stuck in your throat,
Snuffing out your life while helplessly you watch.

But is Africa, a fool?
That sells her children into captivity
Exchanging the product of her conception
With a little ration,
Selling her offspring for food
which is digested to waste.
Oh mother, of enormous wisdom!
Who made you to sink so low?

Where are your scholars, O Africa?
Your great scholars of old
Chinua Achebe, Elechi Amadi,
Ali Alamin Mazrui, Wole Soyinka,
Kenneth David Kaunda, Ngugi wa Thiong'o
Simon Mwansa Kapwepwe, Mpundu Mutale
That they may gather and mourn
That they may proclaim a dirge
Over her loss of direction and future
And grieve for our cruelty
Our foolish insinuations,
driven by selfishness and greed.

Ever heard of a mother who sold her children?
Ever heard of one who sent away her virgin daughter?
To be fondled by evil men afar
Whose appetite and lusts can never be quenched
Nor would their lustful eyes ever be satisfied.

Her sons and daughters are now perpetual beggars;
Their shame, the enemy's crown,
As he continually devises new schemes, keeping me his
      servant
While my mother in deep sleep she is
And her snoring, the enemy's joy.
Because your scholars, like you are asleep
And they interpret not the times
Your children will be servants and slaves forever.
O mother of great understanding!

"Your land has more wine than clean water!" [1]
(Ali Alamin Mazrui, The Africans, 1986).

More cigarettes than farms!
The investors' choice!
Your drunken youth, a sorrowful sight
With a grin, he laughs you to scorn.
Your misery is his joy,
Yet your kings and queens live superfluously
In mansions of cedar and marble;
Lured to append their signatures to bondage
Ascribed on materials they could not fathom
Meticulously shaping doom
for your grandsons and granddaughters,
and you know it not!

CHAPTER 2

AN EXTERNAL FORCE YOU HAVE TO CONTEND WITH!

Who shall roll away this pain from my heart,
Oh mother, of great knowledge?
Who shall wipe away my tears?
My sweat continues to build another man's house,
While on leftovers I live.
A fault not of my own,
Oh, mother of enormous wisdom!

I overheard them say,
"This course was destined for her!"
For a purpose it was crafted,
With malice it was designed,
That a servant for generations I may be
Cushioning off and subsidizing my neighbour's life
That in luxury he may live,
And in despondency and perpetual need I may dwell.

Won't you hear my cry
and come to my rescue?
Didn't your intuition tell you?
Didn't you see them take a whisper
one to the other?
And winked with their eyes

one to another?
Orchestrating a plan of ostracizing you
and your children's children!
That to the grave in sorrow you may go,
And with a seal of approval you may be escorted
While your inheritance is forfeited.

They called it a "Union!"
Something like a Bank too!
No! It sounded like an "International Fund!"
So, they said!
My little learning comprehended it not,
Their smooth and charming talk!

No! They also called it the "International Monetary
      Fund, IMF,"
and the "World Bank!"
"Structural Adjustment Programme, (SAP)" for Africa!
Programmes that have strangled me,
O mother of great understanding!
A modern form of slavery they are!
A new covert machinery of enslavement.
A proclamation of emancipation was done
Since it was overt, everyone knew slavery was evil.
It perpetrated degradation of human beings by others,
At the expense of the so-called, "the elite!"
But somebody said, "All men are born equal!"
"All men needed to be guaranteed the unalienable rights
      of life,
liberty and the pursuit of happiness," [2] (ushistory.org
      July, 1995).

For if in human rights we truly believe,
If in human dignity we delight,
Then, all humans we should have valued
Justice for all nations we should have sought,
That all men were to be granted their unalienable rights
    of life,
liberty, and the pursuit of happiness,
regardless of ethnicity, colour, and nationality!
Alas! So, we believed it were!

Another path we chose,
Another route we took,
That it would go well with us and our children.
After all nature tells us
"It is the survival of the fittest!"
"Scheme after scheme to destroy, enslave, manipulate,
    and rob
we shall employ!"
Effectively annihilating and destroying Africa's hope to
    rise
An advantage created for ourselves
An exploitation unfathomed.

Who shall know of it?
Every learned son and daughter of Africa
we shall indoctrinate,
that nothing good can come out of her.
"No! Not Africa!" we shall say.
We shall also make them believe
that they are a second-class citizen of the world!
No, "Third World!"

(that is why across our world we never grant them equal
      pay for equal job
Whether they be scientists or professionals of any kind!)

We shall coin a name for them!
"Third World" we shall call them!
We shall also wage war against them.
It is a psychological warfare,
For it is able to break even the strongest!
See what it has done to the former slaves' children!

"They are ignorant we shall tell them.
They are incapable we shall repeat!
We shall not show cities and any development
about them (Africa).
We shall beam only the negatives!
We shall make everybody believe
they live in trees, in caves!
Eventually they shall not believe in themselves
And they will be finished as a people."

"We will make them dependent
and not independent.
Whoever discovers this plot
Buy him to us!
Convert him!
Bring him over to us.
Enrich him and let him think like us!
Then he shall not proclaim to others,
Our treasured secrets
If he resists – Take his life!

"After all, it is better for us that one man die for the
        people
than that the whole *of our* nation perish!" [3]
(The Holy Bible, John 11:50 NIV, 1984).

"We will give 'em estrogen, microgynon,
spermicides, condoms, diaphragms
and intrauterine devices (IUD!)
in the name of birth control promotions!
Our efforts and campaigns shall vigorously be targeted
At governments and through non-governmental
        organizations (NGOs).
Check Africa's parity!
Planned Parenthood Association, goodwill for Africa,
        shall be!
After all this will cut down even their numbers
our long-treasured goal it always has been
A secret we have fashioned even here at home!"

Vaccines, we will give them
Our secret not to tell
Systematically, their people to wipe away
Disease to spread clandestinely!
Their land, our inheritance to be
And their numbers to control!

A cry of a mother!
And a cry of her son!
His would-have been brothers and sisters never to see!
For his mother, at 14, was numbered among the victims
of our bitter past history, –
Sterilized at age 14, Elaine Riddick,

her son, siblings never to see!
Unknown then that her only son she gave birth to in 1968
was the only one she was to hold!

Though a product of rape her son was,
her tubes were to be obliterated at delivery!
Sterilized against her will by the elite and not by thugs,
only to discover at 19 in her marriage
that a victim of the U.S. eugenics laws she was!
Laws which persisted into the 1970s!
Enshrined to the parity of the minority like me!
A fate once suffered by the Israelites in Egypt
In Germany, not to mention!
A subtle and stealth population control
By the "elite" upon the common.

"Other states in America," you were told
"Sterilization laws focused mainly on criminals
and people in mental institutions!"
But North Carolina and some other states
the poor to cut open against their will!
"A way to limit public costs!" you were told
Thousands of your women coerced by social workers
"Operation to undergo or risk the loss of public
        assistance!"[4] (Julie Rose, June 22, 2011).
Eugenics at work!

Tulsa, Oklahoma we mourn!
The 1921 Race Massacre we remember!
Nevertheless, in his history books not to write!
Historians deliberately hushed!
No record of the massacre to find!

The annihilation of a people through lynching and
   murders!
Black Wall Street success story of Africans – a story
   untold!
Incendiary bombs dropped on you
to annihilate your successful business story and your
   economics.
Your zeal to defend and protect yourself from accusation
Is greeted with a war on you, carried out by veterans
   from war – World War I!
Yet a racist-prone Government – a defenceless people
   not to protect!
Black Wall Street demolished and over 300 Blacks killed!
A common story you share but they question you
when you say "Black Lives Matter!"
A quest they force you not to pursue!

Bronx Zoo in 2020 apologises!
They apologise for the 1906's putting of a Central
   African man on display in a zoo with monkeys!
Put on exhibition for 20 days in September of 1906
Ota Benga from Congo we mourn you!
Zoo officials today term it "Unconscionable racial
   intolerance!"
Benga is reportedly to have committed suicide in
   Virginia in 1916
A kind of trauma common to us all
On George Floyd's neck they knee – our necks have
   been pinned down with their knees for centuries!
Economic saboteurs' knees on Africans and African
   economies' necks

And Africans sigh, wondering why they are not
      numbered among the list of the holocaust victims
      that the world is familiar with!
The list they created!
– The Police – the new KKK with a badge, enforcing
      legalised lynching
and in the U.S., scot-free they go!

For it is not just the Jews who suffered at the hands of
      Germany!
Germany atrocities on Africans never heralded!
Sterilization of your people in Germany
A genocide of your race at the hands of Germany
in South West Africa never told!
For Africa suffered under the Nazis too!
Many, like the Jewish community in cold blood were
      murdered!
In South West Africa (Namibia) you were slaughtered by
      the Germans
who had trekked into your land
Tanzania, not to forget
Dehumanised and humiliated
"Monkeys" they called you
Guinea pigs for medical experiments you were
A story not told!
Africa, we mourn.
Africa we remember!

Now a new form of eugenics is in existence
A different form that Mother Africa can't see!
Crafted by the intelligentsias of this world
And Africa duped to believe that it is a fallacy

For if you doubt of its existence
then, blind you are!
For the vast issues and challenges you now face
Come packaged in the old but new form of eugenics!
"Economic and social eugenics" now surround you
Like an umbilical cord that encircles a child at birth
Only at the mercy of a highly trained hand to unravel
For death and misery loom at your doorsteps!
Only the wise and the discerning
Can unravel this covert deceit!

"Never allow 'em to take care of themselves
and their offspring," they have conspired,
"That could be dangerous!
More population, more power,
Less population, less power!"
They have known!

"Do not level the playing ground –
That is suicidal.
Attack and attack their minds
Finally, they will break down!
Let us continue with our superiority complex
And we hit and torment them with an inferiority
        complex
It will eat 'em up like moth!
It will disintegrate 'em.
Show only the good about us
(You know we have terrible things too)
But do not let 'em know.
Then they will lose confidence in themselves
as a people."

"Another weapon we shall employ:
'Divide and Rule'
You know it pays off very well.
It has been our greatest weapon
And it has never been known to fail!
Remember how we colonized and ruled?
Somewhere even the Son of Man quoted it!
He said, 'A house divided by itself cannot stand!'[5] (The
        Holy Bible, Mark 3:25 NIV, 1984).
Take opportunity of any internal squabbles and strife!
As you know they are blessed with many tongues!
Read, watch and study the situation!
Pounce on 'em and strike!
With your most deadly poison inflict.
Supply one faction with arms and then that is it!"

"The minority empower,
the majority destroy.
Seeds of animosity to plant forever.
No machinery is too good to diffuse this destructive force
We have succeeded everywhere we introduced it
Biafra, Rhodesia, South Africa, Congo DR, Rwanda,
        Burundi, Iraq, an endless list.
A bloody unavoidable conflict imputed
For centuries never to be obliterated,
An endless dispute that shifts attention
from real issues that require development."

"We have the capabilities to stop these conflicts
But that would not be in our interest
For we would stand to lose
How then could we milk the cow if that were done?"

"We have secured places in many of these regions
controlled by faction groups!
Our birds can land and fly out of these destinations!
Smuggling precious stones.
Any threat against us is met with the strongest resistance
        possible!
We ask governments to cooperate with rebels
(A thing our governments have a zero tolerance for, very
        smart hey!)
To be more tolerant to opposition
and exercise maximum observance of 'human rights!'
Any other government that sees
a just cause and distress of another incumbent
        government
and wishes to render and mobilize support for them
to bring down or crush any uprising is sternly advised to
        keep away!"

"We tell 'em you have seen nothing!
We flex our muscles against any antagonist
We vehemently call them 'communists!'
And none would dare, you know!
This we did against Robert Mugabe of Zimbabwe
and Sam Nujoma of Namibia when together forces they
        joined.
To offer support to a beleaguered Laurent Kabila's
        Congo DR!
That Laurent Kabila's beleaguered Congo DR forces
        support they may get
A threat on them we announced,
But Uganda as you know,
(ruled by Museveni for more than 28 years, an ally she is!),

Rwanda and Burundi with worst genocide records in
    history
second only to Hitler against the Jews,
illegally in Congo DR at our cost we let them institute a
    carnage!
Them, never to condemn!
For very important to us is the region they occupy in
    Congo DR!
'Our Interest,' we call it!"

"In case you seem surprised and confused
Like a tale this to you sounds.
Then remember that when the nation of Congo DR
our long-time ally was losing grip
in despair, we found ourselves!
Diagnosed with prostate cancer,
The General who had ruled Congo DR
(then Zaire, a very wealthy African nation the size of
    Western Europe)
Who we never bothered
that free and fair elections he could hold,
As we do/were doing to Mugabe,
A time to play another *trump* card had come for Central
    Africa!
Do you smell the rat?"

"When terminally ill, therefore, he fell
And an eminent loss of control we saw
We immediately did what we always do
The next bet to find
A rebel soldier we had to find
Unmindful to us that a *rebel* he had been

As long as the cow we would continue to milk
That for us is sufficient
For we care less!
'Our own interest,' in the region to keep and pursue!
(In case this too you doubt,
recall that in Libya rebels we supported too
That Gaddafi would go!)"

"Laurent had meanwhile mobilized himself well.
His uprising more support had gained!
Besides, an English speaker in a French-speaking
        country he was!
The best bet on him, therefore, we had!
And so, camp we switched!
To rally behind him a new promise we gave!
With the might dollar, like the rest of them all to lure!
And yes, he did win!
Though by way of a military campaign it came – little
        did we care!
Smelt another dead rat?
This game we have perfected for centuries!"

"The death of Dictator Mobutu Sese Seko
who had supplied us with all that we had needed
turned out to be a nightmare to our cause!
So, desperate we had become
that another ally who could be as foolish as him we needed!
That the enormously rich and vast African cow we
        would continue to milk!
I am afraid to inform you that our cards
were not played right when we offered our support
to President Laurent Kabila!

He could not negotiate nor could he part away
with his (*our*) minerals!"

"An opportunity, however, presented itself for us!
An uprising!
During his campaign to dislodge a onetime invincible
      Mobutu,
He had used foreign rebels from Uganda, Rwanda, and
      Burundi.
Backpedalling on his earlier promise
of giving them government and ministerial jobs brought
      about
a mutiny to which he was never going to recover.
We heard he was not going to incorporate
the foreign rebels into his government
despite having helped him dislodge Mobutu!
(We had used them before to help keep Mobutu in
      power perpetually!)
He (Kabila) had succeeded within a short period to
      repair the damage
we had caused for decades!
Rebuilding a country damaged by the dictator!
(I hate to use this term to an African leader!)
We could not just lose our money that we pumped in
(as you are already aware by now that it is not for free,
it always has to bring in dividends in one way or another
and that is the goodness of capitalism, you know!)"

"But a certain highly eloquent and ambitious
      Zimbabwean
leader is very stubborn!

He refuses to heed our instructions and advice to keep
  out of Congo DR!
We were directly and openly in support of those who
  were in rebellion
trying to remove Kabila!
But this eloquent leader from the 'Ruins of Zimbabwe'
  mustn't dare us!
Already he wants to redistribute his (Zimbabwean) land
to his natives.
Just because we did not honour the clause of
  redistributing the land
in 20 years' time
As signed in the Lancaster Agreement that paved a way
  for Southern Rhodesia's independence
Therefore, after 20 years of Independence!
Let's hurt him then!"

"All his assets in Europe are frozen with immediate effect
All his members of cabinet
and their families are barred from visiting or shopping in
  Europe!
(Note: like a teacher telling an errant and truant
  kindergarten child!)
The exchange rate has plummeted too!
This will be so because his elections were 'not fair!'
(Oh, we mean that at least not as fair as
the Al Gore-President George Bush one!)
And he deported one of our reporters!
Do not talk about those thousands who we deport!"

"Even our UN birds cannot be questioned!
No government worth its salt

Would dare inspect our birds flying into these
     destinations.
They are on "official UN missions" you know!
We did it in Congo DR![6]
A three days' stand-off finally worked for us!
Kabila could not inspect our bird that he had grounded at
Kinshasa International Airport!
The poor African did not know what he was playing
     with!"

How can the Mother of all Evil
(sorry, the Mother of all Righteousness)
going into a government's enemy-controlled territory,
a place endowed with great mineral wealth,
with nothing to hide,
refuse its cargo to be inspected
when ordered by a ruling government
before proceeding into the enemy zone?

"We are extortionists, plunderers and rapists
of the African economy,
Even under the keen eye of UN peacekeepers
Arms to factions we sell and gold and diamonds we
     collect!
A long haul we are in!
And this we call, 'Peacekeeping Mission!'
But let no one know this
For no mortal man dare have knowledge of this!
'Partners in development!'
We would rather they assumed."

Bosco Ntanganda alias "The Terminator"

A Rwandese rebel courted by the elite
An independent nation of Congo DR he chooses to
     destabilize
Under the watchful eye of Washington,
the UN not to mention,
sanctions against the rebels not to enforce!
A free pass between Congo DR and Rwanda daily
not to punish,
For highly lucrative is the war that maims
and destroys both property and human life.
Kivu, Eastern Congo we mourn
Kagame, bloody money to benefit
Minority to rule only under evil-hearted allies
The Belgians' long lop-sidedness of past policy to
     emulate
Mark Doyle's herald to civilized nations not to heed!
A UN report's release blocked by the self-proclaimed
"champions of democracy!"[7] (Mark Doyle BBC News
     Africa, 21 June, 2012).

"We do not show our true colours
That is why those who discover who we really are
are dangerous to our national survival, interests,
and existence as a nation:
They are communists and they should not be permitted
     to live."
This explains the rationale for the 26 years' Angolan War
1.5 million people dead and over 70,000 maimed,
South African liberation struggle and apartheid
     over 21,000 killed and over 18,000 arrested or
     imprisoned.

Libya air strikes and isolation, hundreds killed and
    millions affected.
Congo DR, now over 10 million people dead.
Cross border destabilization of independent African
    countries
such as Zambia during Southern Africa liberation with
    hundreds killed.
Turning your land into weapons' test zone!
While his remains secure!

What more?
I have no time to explain to you about the Biafra war in
    Nigeria,
Somalia, Sierra Leone, Liberia, Ivory Coast, Eritrea,
    Algeria, Libya!
This also explains the justification for Vietnam,
    Afghanistan,
Iraq, Haiti, the Falkland Islands, an endless list!

"But if the UN headquarters were in Africa, or Cuba
And one of their birds were to come to our countries
'on official visits,'
they would be subjected to inspection!
Failure to comply would be deemed as conspiracy and
    treason!
Double standards … ee!
For we are always right and so is our point of view!"

"Third World!" we shall call them!
But I was born a citizen,
I was born free,
I was born on the same planet – earth

Like you, we all have equal rights to this earth
"Because the earth is the Lord's
and everything in it,
the world, and all who live in it," [8] (The Holy Bible
      Psalm 24:1 NIV, 1984).
Didn't you know that the world is one,
Oh mother, Africa?
Didn't you know you too have equal rights
to enter all countries as they do to you?

Somebody said, "All animals are equal," [9] (George
      Orwell, 1945).
Indeed, some appear to be more equal
than others!
Your people lie massacred in cold blood
Your leaders instruct your people to tighten
their belts
In anticipation of harder times ahead
Yet theirs remain loosed!
They are political stooges of their masters
Carrying out instructions of your enemy
Even your enemy's belt is never tightened
He wallows in plenty while you swim in poverty
and shame.

An external force you ought to see
An external force too powerful,
too shrewd to see!
But your Maker, eyes he shall give you
Wisdom he shall grant you
Your sons and daughters not only shall they contend
with it,

Charles Kapungwe

but an oppressive regime
soon they shall dismantle!

CHAPTER 3

Awake from Your Slumber O Africa!

Won't you awake from your slumber?
Throughout their lives
Your sons and daughters know nothing
but rationing.
Rationing for food;
They could not believe if you told them that somewhere
on the same planet
when your children fight to put on flesh on their
        emaciated bodies
Their friend is fighting to shed off extra pounds!
A paradox of fate and justice.

Food! A weapon he uses to enslave you!
Why spend time at the watering hole?
Your strength at something that will destroy you?
Sipping countless bottles of liquor
Putting your mind to sleep
That an illusion you may carry
For a dull mind will not perceive
Nor could it ponder a way out of the maze
That you have been driven into
For only wisdom and learning will take you out.

Charles Kapungwe

Your enemy, the instigator of violence
Among your people
Watches from afar
Grinning with approval
As you set yourselves ablaze
Killing yourselves shamelessly
Brother against brother
And sister against sister.

What have you done Rwanda?
What have you allowed to happen Burundi?
What about you Congo DR, Sierra Leone,
Nigeria, Angola, South Africa, Sudan.
How about you Ethiopia, Eritrea, Somalia,
Congo Brazzaville, Central African Republic, Mauritania,
Mali, Algeria, Libya, Tunisia, Egypt, Liberia,
Burkina Faso, Togo and Ivory Coast?

You have annihilated your own people, Sudan,
You have maimed your own sons and daughters, Angola,
You have killed your own flesh and blood:
Rwanda, Burundi, Congo DR, Libya, Mali, Egypt
You have swallowed up your children Ivory Coast,
        Senegal
You have destroyed your own kinsmen Ethiopia,
        Somalia, Eritrea
You have cut off your own strength, Uganda
You have destroyed your own family Sierra Leone, Togo,
        Liberia!
You have killed your own blood South Africa!
Visitors to your beautiful land from within Africa
are now deemed your enemy!

To the grave shall your shame follow you
Your folly never to be atoned for
For to be fools you chose
Wicked, stubborn, and heartless fools you chose to be
For knowledge and wisdom to the dogs you threw
Refusing to receive correction, advice, and understanding
Spilling of innocent blood, you found delight in.
In guilt and shame to the grave you shall go;
Folly and shame your rampart forever to be.

Why sell your people?
No! That is "His-story!"
For some Arabs and Europeans came
and rounded up your people!
Leaving a little gunpowder and cloth for you,
as they left with your people,
claiming that "You had sold them your people!"
Letting your peace go to the wind
Which you once cherished,
At the time, you lived in harmony one with the other
An external threat you knew not,
Nor did you need to keep vigil all night long
For a cruel animal on two feet
Except for those with hind legs
Which too were friendly to you
Oh, mother of the jungle!

Why are you insensitive?
Oh, mother of civilisation?
Why don't you learn from your neighbours?
Learn from history!
They have supported insurgencies

All over the world!
Yet they are champions of democracy!
They have paid disgruntled elements among nations
Who they have supported to topple governments!
Away from their homes!

But there are women and children
Even in these nations
Who suffer and cry during such calamities –
Champions of human rights!
They say they care for peace;
They care for life.
No, not when they need your wealth
Remember Panama, The Falklands, Nicaragua, Cuba,
      Grenada,
Taiwan, Afghanistan, the Soviet Union, Bosnia
      Herzegovina,
Pakistan (once a foe now a friend), Iraq!

Then your own South Africa, Zimbabwe,
Angola, Mozambique, Namibia, Congo DR, Nigeria,
Liberia, Sierra Leone, Libya, Sudan, Ivory Coast, Congo
      Brazzaville,
An endless list!
What price could you have paid if the opposite were the
      case?
What could the cost have been for you
If you rose up against the tyrannies
Who mistreat people of your descent in their nations?
If you told them to democratize!
If, like them, you planted seeds of rebellion and
      disobedience

In the name of fighting for equality?

Africa believes Taiwan and China are one,
Hawaii and America are one,
And Argentina and The Falkland Islands are one!
And so are Russia, "Yugoslavia," Germany, Korea,
	Vietnam, UK,
or Sudan!
But alas Sudan you who annihilate your own people!
A divided nation you now are!

No, you are not dull!
You can read and discern
Who is your true neighbour?
Your true friend?
There is no such a thing as sovereignty,
That word is not in his dictionary,
When it concerns you!
But is applicable to herself
Double standards!
Don't ever attack her sovereignty
It will cost you dearly!
Your women and children will be ripped open
Your men will be sent scampering in all directions!

Why does your labour always fail to pay off?
Your years of toil are never rewarded!
You said, "I will work hard to feed my children.
I shall ensure that they eat bread and butter
and they drink tea with milk.
Their table shall lack nothing.
I will provide for them

like a responsible mother
so that none of my children
shall be destitute and beggars
in the land of their ancestors."

But mother this has been your elusive dream!
An unfulfilled dream it has been,
Carefully planned and created by your master
For you to live an unfulfilled dream!
To be a laughingstock among your peers
Who scorn at your failures
and denounce you for faults
not of your own-making
As you cry and bemoan your state
of helplessness, hopelessness, and haplessness!

Your years of labour yield nothing
Your enemy encircles you
And you know it not!
The look in your face is that of innocence
Like a child whose knowledge is all engraved in the
        mother
As a supplier of all its needs
Unaware of an external evil at the doorway,
A ferocious beast at your doorsteps
So, you are!

Your enemy determines your profits
And your ration
Your economy is in another man's hand
"Your exchange rate is poor"
So, he tells you!

Your learned sons and daughters
Fail to reconcile the disparity
Why in poverty you wallow in the midst of riches!
They cannot fathom this perpetual plan
Orchestrated against you and your children.

Your hard work never produces an economic growth!
Your effort and toil go down the drain,
A painful experience for you and your womb,
Who says this experience is not painful?
Who says you shall remain still and not talk back?
Who says you shall die in this state of despair and
        despondency?
No! I am not inferior because I was born this side
of the world!
Across the oceans
In the land, you called "Africa!"
No! I am like this because the playing ground
has not been levelled!
Try to level the playing ground and you will
soon see and discover what I am made of!

Melanin is not the determinant factor of one's
        intelligence
Nor is a place of birth proof of one's capabilities.
When will you ever cease to judge me by the colour of
        my skin
And begin to judge me rightly,
By the content of my character?[10] (Dr. Martin Luther
        King, Jr. "I have a dream," 1963).
And when will you cease from your endless stereotype
That has characterized your life

Ever since we knew you?
You have continuously said, "From Africa!"
"No, African!"
"Can anything good come out of Africa?" you always ask.

I bemoan your wrongly perceived lack
Your meticulously designed mess
That your leaders fail to undo
Years of trial and error not enough
To unbuckle knots of tightly sealed bundles
Of economic malaise,
Whose blueprint lies far away from you
A secret kept from you for decades
A call made by your technocrats to discover
But to no avail always it has been.

You have been used, misused, and abused
O mother of abundance!
Your forefathers were banished from their land
Your fathers were exploited and oppressed
Now your sons and daughters
continue to bear the consequences
not of their own-making!

Your enemy's aid, gifts, and donations
are repugnant, highly nauseating
Given with conditions attached,
They sharply contrast that sacrificial gift,
The Lamb of God,
Given unconditionally to mankind
By the Almighty God,
To be a propitiation for our sins

An atonement and sacrifice
of unfailing love
Given as a pattern for all mankind's giving.

And now a new calamity sweeps over you!
It is something your ancestors never heard of
or experienced before
It is the dreaded news of death
Your mortuaries swell with your people
Your young ones and old
Your graves and cemeteries
Increase their cruel hold
Never letting go of your loved ones
They call it a "Disease of the immune system!"

Is it a God-sent disease?
Is it a man-sent disease?
Or is it a devil-sent disease?
I overheard them say,
"We can have their inheritance, like flies they are dying!"
Was it engineered in the lab?
Was it a result of our promiscuity?
But they are more promiscuous than you O Africa!
Is life unfair?
Why had it to be you?
To bear the consequences of evil heartedness of man.

Your sons and daughters keep on dying in my hands
They call upon me to attend to them
One by one they come to me
I prescribe this drug
I give them that but all to no avail

They keep on wasting away
'Till the cold hand of death
Grasps them heavily away
Never letting them have a break.

They go, leaving their loved ones
A long list of victims, he claims
Misery and mourning mark your people
Who can count the widows?
Nor the number of your orphans?
The numbers continue to multiply
An endless list leading to the grave
Your children weep
Your women beat their chests
At the loss of their loved ones
As the grave continues to swallow your people
Unsatisfied still needing more
Who can count the slain among you?
Nor the numbers of those afflicted?

When will you come to your senses?
O mother of dignitaries?
That unless you produce more food for yourself
and your offspring
Surplus food to store
Your shame will never leave you
For you were born not to be a perpetual beggar
But to be kings and queens, sons and daughters
Because you are from the royal family
Do not let anyone belittle you!

I know you shall rise above your problems

You shall overcome your frustrations
They shall not overwhelm you forever.
The challenges were meant to strengthen you
To make you discover your full potential
Your ability to rise above your failures.
Soon you shall carry that which carried you
And refuse to succumb to its demands.

Why do you listen to your enemy,
when he plants seeds of animosity among you?
Why do you accept a bribe?
All you children of disobedience
Accepting a bribe that makes you turn a blind eye
Bloody money that finances civil disobedience
That they call "Opposition!"

All you children of an adulterous mother
And a promiscuous father
Were you brought forth to give opposition to your
        leaders?
Making your territories ungovernable
Or were you given birth to render help to your leaders,
That they may govern your people well?
Then you may enjoy peace and tranquillity
That mother Africa was given.

You are a teacher of hatred,
So, I hear someone say to me!
Ignore him, he is a child void of understanding
But I am tired of always listening from "his point of view"
A slanted voice of reason
That never shares my plight

Nor the cry of my mother Africa and her children
For the grip I bear, is the grip of death
And the burden I shoulder, is a burden of oppression
So, heavy has been the grip on me and my children
A choking grip it has been
Meant to suffocate me to death!

My enemy's currency is ever gaining in strength
While that of my children continue to plummet daily!
2,500,000 plus Congolese (Zairean) francs currency to
    1 US dollar
So, they tell me!
My son President Laurent Kabila refuses to accept it
He cries foul
My son insists Congolese Francs (CDF) to 1 US dollar
He cannot see why his mineral-rich territory
should be poor!
He cannot relent to pressure
nor could he change his mind on principle
So, it costs his life!
They send him to the grave
And make me believe they are innocent
in the shedding of his blood.

Zimbabwe! O Zimbabwe!
"The highest inflation rate in the world!"
In billions your currency lies devalued
Sanctions and poverty, your necklaces
For in audacity and defiance you stood
In courage, you opposed perceived injustice
And in punishment boldly you stood,
Because suffering for what was right you believed in

That "Unearned suffering was redemptive," [10] (Dr.
    Martin Luther King, Jr. "I have a dream," 1963).
So, you heard your leader Martin Luther King, Jr. tell you
And you echoed his voice
In danger and in death
Still you rise up!

CHAPTER 4
AFRICA:
THE BATTLEFIELD
FOR RESOURCES,
POWER AND CONTROL!

Africa, Mother Africa!
The battlefield for superpowers
Who care less at the number of the slain
Unmoved by your pain and anguish
As long as your wealth they tap
Enriching themselves while blood they shed
That their businesses at home and abroad they may run
Driven by drenched sweat and spilled blood of your
    children
Her wealth snatched and sent miles afar
While to fight hunger, disease, and turmoil you are left
Deliberately left behind by your adversary.

Rebels from Rwanda, Burundi, and Uganda
Supported by the British and US governments
Without shame or remorse once again tear down
And ruin a country:
Masters at killing other peoples' independence and
    sovereignty
Planting once again seeds of destabilization and disunity
    for gain

Remember, in the same country soon after
      independence
From the Belgians, Congo and Africa lost a powerful
      leader
In the name of Patrice Lumumba
The same dirty hands carried out the mission
Thanks to the CIA conspiracy, [11] (The Washington Post,
      June 27, 2007).

When evil men who are part of the conspiracy
To take one of my territories – Congo DR
Africa's sons protest at the injustice
perpetrated by the rich and exploiters of Africa's
      resources.
Zimbabwe and Namibia line up their armies
to defend the incumbent President
"Champions of democracy" tell Zimbabwe and Namibia
to keep away!
While other political stooges lie in wait
to harm a sovereign state
What hypocrisy!
But what are my other sons Uganda,
Rwanda, and Burundi doing in Congo DR
and you have not said anything to them?

You control the diamond-rich territory, your interest!
Do you think I will ever trust you?
Should all African states stay akimbo?
While one of my sons remains embattled
By forces of evil
That they may share the spoils!
You have been dehumanized

O mother Africa!

Libya, O Libya!
Your oil spoils now to share!
Your enthusiasm, Africa to unite
Your downfall to ensure!
Rebels "UN" to support!
Her mandate of her formation quickly forgotten!
Incumbent government and a sovereign nation to
        dislodge!
And in silence the rest of the world watches
As "NATO" destroys my son!
Muammar Gaddafi's ambitious Programme of
        empowering Africa to shred!
Africa's telecommunication vision to free her
from exorbitant routing, European and American
        surcharges
at the heart of this carnage
And oil resources the final goal to acquire
"A united Africa" vision-bearer to snuff out
"And a dictator to remove"
So, goes "his" story!

Your enemy has degraded and humiliated you;
He has made you sit akimbo
As you try to figure out your destiny.
Sorrow and desperation your countenance,
Your past has been obliterated
Your present has been destroyed,
And your future painted bleak
And a lie you have been made to believe.

Every day is sorrow after sorrow for you.
As the first rays hit your windows
You are awakened to another new day, –
A day of hopelessness and despair.
Will you ever put food on your table? you ask.
Will your children continue to be haunted by your
    enemy?
He has disguised the problem you now face
For he calls it "inflation!"

Inflation has tormented you,
O mother of great riches!
It is the scapegoat for your poverty
A front that has been paraded
To disguise you from reality,
To make my mother blind to real issues!
As she is made to wander in a maze of mediocrity
A laughingstock of her tormentors!

"Would she ever awake from her slumber?"
they ask,
"Would she ever discover our plans?"
they inquire,
Why don't you awake and see?
Your destiny has been masterminded
By people who are ruthless
They force you to tighten your belts
Which have constricted your waists
You constantly stoop and can now hardly straighten up!
For your stomach aches
And your knees are feeble.

But your men were short-sighted
Your nationalists could not perceive.
Apartheid they saw,
And discrimination they saw,
But another powerful enemy lay in wait:
Neo-colonialism.
It is an economical slavery
It is as oppressive as the former
But your children say the latter is worse off!
Exploitation of man by man!
It has bred corruption, prostitution, hunger, and disease.
Who said, "Africa we are independent?"

Who shall deliver us, O mother?
Will your young men and women
dismantle the oppressors' victory?
Call upon all Africa's technocrats
Young men and women of understanding
A new breed of freedom fighters
From east to west
And from north to south, they shall come
To plan an assault on the common enemy
No spirit of liberation can be broken
Nor can it be buried.

Kwame freed his people
Neto, Kaunda, Nyerere, Samora, Kamuzu,
Nujoma, Nkomo, Mugabe, Kenyatta
And Mandela did it too
27 years of prison could not break his spirit
An example of African strength
That baffles the oppressor.

Oranjemund, Namibia, a diamond-rich territory of yours!
An embargo against you is imposed,
Through South Africa, your land Namibia only to
    access!
The story that Africa is familiar with! Liberia, her rich
    diamonds, locals not reach!
Somalia, your wealth they pilfer from your rich coastline
And you know it not!
Deposits of mineral wealth in your sand
Unheralded to you!

Your charcoal made from acacia trees,
charcoal from Somalia, a highly valued commodity
in the Gulf nations because of its sweet aroma
A sweet aroma it gives to grilled meats
and to tobacco burned in waterpipes
from your land, it is siphoned!

Your enemy laughs at you,
as your leaders go around and around
In an endless cycle
To find a cure for Africa's economic malaise.
He grins at you
As he sees an impossible task you carry
For in his crafty hands lies the solution
Yet he would never let go
That Africa's children would prosper and be free.
But the One above who holds the universe laughs
At the evil of man
For he shall soon shake the earth
And he who puts trust in mortal man will be dismayed
    and disdained.

Your children have been molested
Your women taken from your men
And your men taken from your women
Wooed by your enemy's wealth
As your sons watched helplessly
At the insinuations of your enemy
As he takes away your pride
Touching you were it gives pain most
Leaving you bewildered and in shame.

"Shut up!" you tell me?
"You man of hatred
casting nothing but violence,
Preacher of hatred and vengeance."
No, I'm not!
An educator I am,
An informer of my people
Of the evils that man can do
The oppression and injustice
That mortal man can harbour
Aiming it at his fellow man.

Malcolm X was an instigator in life
But a hero after his death!
Dr. Martin Luther King, Jr., was a villain in life
But a "hero" for the cause of justice after his death!
I heard someone say, "If a man deserves praise
give it to him now, for he will not be there to read his
    tombstone." [12] (Anonymous).
Accolades too wonderful, given too late!
King was a voice of justice, and so was Malcolm

Of "hate that hate produced!" [13] (The Autobiography of
    Malcolm X, 1965).
Indira Gandhi, Steve Biko all shouted:
"Justice, justice, let there be justice!"
The assassins' hands could not let them live!

Every voice that wants to speak for the oppressed
often end in a pool of blood
The oppressors never want to listen to the voice of
    reason
The Son of Man they crucified too!
President John F. Kennedy,
Swedish Prime Minister Olof Palme, among victims
But a voice they could not silence
Nor could your will be broken
Because Africa beams with love
The love that hate failed to quench
The love that Love produced
It is not the love of this world
But the love from above.

Brace for a new leadership
A well-versed leadership
A leadership full of the Spirit of God
That shall dismantle the shackles of oppression
And break the mouths of young lions
For no kingdom lasts forever but One
So, says history!
The Babylonian Empire crashed
The Roman Empire crumbled
The British Empire tumbled
The Soviet Union collapsed

And so, shall neo-colonialism and imperialism
And Africa shall, indeed, be free!

Have you ever felt the pain?
Or experienced the pain
When you were pledged to get married to your
        wonderful woman,
your beautiful virgin
A would-be wife of your youth
Then from nowhere and suddenly
Someone else snatched her from you?
Have you ever experienced the pain
of not having a place to call your home?
A nomad you are
"Homeless," they call you!
A choice not of your own
Orchestrated by your enemy to destroy you.

The cold engulfs you in the night,
The sun scorches you by the day,
"Destitute" they call you!
A laughingstock of your fellow man
Who publishes and exposes your shame and sorrow
Your skinny, wasted, and emaciated bodies of your
        children
are his delight.
"Ethiopia," they say,
"Somalia," they call.
"Sudan, The Lost Boys!" they tease.
Something not of your own-making, O mother!

"O ye foolish and ignorant writer!"

So, they tell me, O mother!
"You ignorant and an uneducated race!
Is it me who kills your people
when they rise up against one another?
Shooting at one another?
Wiping out themselves like mad people
and their bodies lie sprawled like flies?"

"But who supplies me with guns?"
I ask.
"Who takes my diamonds, gold, crude oil
in exchange for killing machines?
Who divides my people and sponsors wars?
Who exports 'democracy' among my people,
an ideology that breeds disrespect,
lack of submission to elders and leadership
and promotes erosion of morals?"
Bringing absolute freedom with the so-called "Human
    Rights!"
Human rights to the homosexual!
Human rights to the lesbian!
Human rights to lawlessness!
Human rights to a child against parental discipline,
A detestable thing and alien to your rich culture,
O mother of great knowledge!

Have you ever felt it?
When you never knew when your next meal would be?
When would your children sit around the table again?
When shall you give the provision to your wife again?
The disgrace of your failure to provide for her
Now, your opponent puts food in her laps

You beautiful daughters are next.

Your daughters are taken to be caressed by your enemy
Exported as though they were goods!
To go and parade for your drunken master
"Dancing queens," they are named
"Commercial Sex Workers," they are tagged!
An embarrassing situation for you.
Your young men are imported
To provide cheap labour
Lured to earn the dollar and the euro
Others remain destitute
They lurk at every corner
From dustbin to dustbin, they go
Trying to find what to put in their empty bellies!

Yes, a few so-called NGOs (Non-Governmental
    Organizations)
are doing something for them
But can you trust them?
They are surrogate institutions of their master
Using your recycled wealth
Now disguised as donation or aid.
Your wealth that your forced labour produced
Derived from your riches
With empty bowls, they go
Forced to beg from their master
And now they entice the masses
To disobey my mother's governance
To please their master
An empty bowl that they may fill again
While he grins again with approval!

That "You live in trees,"
is an insult, unpalatable
That "You live in caves,"
is salt added to injury
O mother of civilisation!
Your enemy is not as wise as you are made to think
His children know little about you, your exploits
Ignorance covers their face
Yet in deceit, he portrays himself wise
But your children are wiser
Geniuses who know more than their contemporaries!

Let no one look down upon you
Let no one deflate your ego
Your understanding, no one can fathom
Your ingenuity who can surpass?

Congo Brazzaville: The untold story!
A story of manipulation and theft
France, Oh France!
Like them all, our colonial masters
Oil to pilfer
Dennis Sassou Nguesso
A stooge for the rich to be
His people to oppress and sell
A sense of reason to the nationalists not to hear
And to war he goes against his people
Backed by another – of Africa's enemies
With Paris to protect
The enemy, oil to benefit cheaply
And timber to pilfer!

Pascal Lissouba, the visionary
Like Robert Mugabe, his people to protect
Mother Africa at heart
His people to help!
For if "With them you cooperate
and wealth to pilfer,
immunity from prosecution, you to be granted!"
And the Kangaroo Court then, you not to touch!

But alas!
The enemy will not let him!
Lissouba's voice to silence, in exile to send.
Because France to pay for oil at market value she was
    asked!
The simple not to understand
The fate that Laurent Kabila found himself in is lurking
    at his doorsteps!
Therefore, he is made to flee!
A genocide in Congo Brazzaville ensues
Dennis Sassou Nguesso backed by a foreign military
    power!
His people to annihilate!
The cruel colonialist, Pascal and his weak nationals to
    crash!
The Tropical Forest is covered with blood
The blood: wheels that drives capitalism
And no herald of the carnage is heard among their
    newscasters!
Ben Bella and Algerian history, not to forget!
Francophone countries in turmoil endlessly they are
Their master, strings never to stop to pull
"Independence" an illusion it is.

And there you are!
Rolling your eyes at me!
"A son of hate you are!" so you tell me.
"Don't you see the help we offer you?"
you mischievously ask me
"Can't you see our men and women on the ground?
Rendering help in every land of your continent?" you
retort:

Well! Far be it from me that your deceit I may buy!
Far be it that I may be bought by stealth work
paraded as a cover up of an uncaring people!
Ever heard of clandestine operations
carried out in every land to benefit them?
Ever heard of clandestine operations that topple
governments?
Then to school please go
Before you could address me again!
"The Bible preceded the gun!" we know
Use of the "Church" they even sometimes do, even
today!
Fear for the Lord, they have not!
The Vatican, other denominations, France – among
innumerable accomplices to some coups:
A development agenda to curb
Chaos to plant forever!
And Africa, to trust you, you still need?

CHAPTER 5
AFRICA:
A TIME TO ARISE!

Your strength is more than that of a horse
Something admired by your peers
He has disgraced me
But I will not give up
Nor will I give in
He has painted me black
But I will not believe his lie!
For I know who I am!
And I know what I can do!

It was like the day I was born
When a group of women uncovered me
"It is a boy!" so they had said
Little did I care
That they saw my shame
For boy, I was
They did for me what I could not do for myself
Yes, for boy I was!

Now a man I am!
I will arise and sit back not
When you parade my shame
You expose me to embarrassment
I will not sit back
When you enemy of mine

Decide to make me a laughingstock
Launching a campaign of ridicule
To shame me before the world
"He is ignorant," you say
"Dull," you claim
"There is nothing good about her," you repeat.

Will I sit back and watch your stupidity?
For man, I am.
Your children have suffered
They are targets of years of oppressive cruelty
Slain by man's brutality
A seemingly endless torture
A yoke that you have carried
Since your slave days
Twilight it has always been
You dream of morning
Yet long hours of darkness greet you
O mother Africa!

You have been objects of his wrath
O mother Africa!
Your sons and daughters embrace forced labour
Against their will
They are recipients of exploitation of man by man
Yet, your resilience has been your pride
The strength that matches a lion
Has been your rampart
Your spirit unbroken
Absorbing years of cruelty and oppression.

Why did they hinder you?

Why did they frustrate you?
Why did they oppress you?
You possess everything that can make you a world leader
All the resources you have
Why didn't you listen to your senior statesmen?
Muammar Gaddafi:
Who saw a United States of Africa!
Or Kwame Nkrumah
Who saw Pan Africanism!

A powerful force to shut your enemies up
A threat to his craft intent
But we are one people
A loving people
No river separated us
No mountain divided us
Nor was any watershed a barrier among us
For one Africa, we had
Africans, we were
Africans, we are
And Africans we shall ever be.

Treaty after treaty
You are made to sign
A wish for you to end your misery
Papers you can't fathom
Flashed into your face,
Your understanding waned
Your vision myopically drugged
Eluded and void of sight
As you fall prey to your adversary forever.

Charles Kapungwe

Tell it not to nations
Announce it not
Lest they hear about your sorrow
Your contentious trap they know
Laughter and mockery
May be heard across the seas
As you fail to hide from your shame
And your cry is heard from afar.

The inequalities and disparities have killed my people
I fail to grasp why it is so
In a world of a global economy
I cannot accept this artificial disproportion
O mother Africa!
It is meant to suffocate and choke you to death
Dying, a slow painful death
At the hands of an unmindful executioner.
Who shall rescue your people from this endless
      bondage?
Who shall break these slavery chains off my ankles and
      wrists?

Shackles of oppression encircle me
I have known no breathing space
Desperation and oppression have been my food for years
I know not peace and freedom
A heavy muzzle covers my mouth
While my enemy watches
A good sight for him and his children
A shameful sight for me, my wife, and children
But does anyone care?
No, not one, because Africa you are!

I cannot believe the disparities
The yawning gap in my economy
An artificial shortage of goods
Created by my enemy
To make me a perpetual beggar and slave
But I was told slavery ended in 1863
So, I was made to believe
But my children continue to be someone's slaves.

"You don't know what you are talking about!"
Don't I?
But I am not as ignorant as you are made to understand!
I am big enough to know and understand.
Who told me to privatize?
Who told me to sell my companies?
And to who?
Obviously to "them!"
When I concede, he strips off my mines' equipment!
He declares my men and women redundant!
A major outcry grips my people!
He closes some companies and they become warehouses
Of imported finished products from other territories!

They even have the audacity of pulling out
of Zambia's mines after stripping them clean!
Aware that they were not obligated to pay for breach of
        contract!
A combination of a crafty bogus investor and oppressor
and my corrupt leaders!
A forced investor upon you to take!

Because your mouth has been in a muzzle

You cannot talk back
O mother Africa!
Your voice cannot be heard!
Your voice is but a groan sound of pain
That none can pay attention to!
Your voice in the UN is a sorrowful noise!
55 nations to your credit
But with no voice!

An instrument of oppression
Hijacked by the enemy
Your suggestion stands to be vetoed!
Vetoed because it is an African reasoning!
You always thought that it was the media for justice
An impartial court for the voiceless and oppressed
But wrong you were:
It is a powerful tool for the affluent
Carrying out orders for your opponent!

One nation features two teams in the World Cup!
Three in the preliminaries!
They become separate states for the sake of the game!
But they are one!
Until recently 54 African nations were only granted one,
        then two,
then three and now five spots!
Let Africa's most populous state of Nigeria
feature four teams in the next soccer World Cup!

1966: The "World" Cup Africa boycotted!
"16 teams only to attend the Finals in England"
– So, FIFA had ruled!

"Ten spots for Europe,
five spots for Latin America and only one spot
Asia, Australia and Africa to compete for!"
Africa, cries! An appeal FIFA could not listen to!
A possible retribution for demanding for independence
        it was,
so Africa thought.
Though many of your countries they had ruled
to put you down had still been their long-cherished
        dream
and bewildered in pain you remained!

A *secret* ballot of the UN General Assembly elects five
        countries to the Security Council!
In June 2019, they included St. Vincent and the
        Grenadines (the smallest nation ever to secure a
        seat), Estonia, Niger, Tunisia and Viet Nam. They
        were earmarked to take up seats in January 2020
        from Cote d'Ivoire, Equatorial Guinea, Kuwait,
        Peru and Poland! "Spectators" to be, to the rubber
        stamp body of the strong!
And none, questions the undemocratic ideals of the
        lopsided body and "enforcer of democratic ideals"
        and tool of the Wicked!

And you are happy O Africa!
Who is it that insults your intelligence?
O mother of nations!
Your wisdom built the pyramids
They defy modern architectural concepts
Sole leaders in writing and in numbers
A hijacked credit by your enemy

In a continued bid to paint you black
But we cannot redo history
For mother Africa is ace in civilisation.

There, the Son of Man lived
To hide from tyrannies
A blessed place of refuge you became
Giving sanctuary to your Creator
The Son and our Father
Affirming to his unchangeable Word:
"Out of Egypt I called my son," [14] (The Holy Bible
      Matthew 2:15 NIV, 1984).

The Light of the World walked on your soil
Leaving an imprint of love
A permanent imprint of Light
But someone erroneously called you "Dark Continent!"
Misnamed you because of his ignorance
Unknown to him was your rich culture and tradition
Disclosed only to the simple.

For there, Your Son found refuge
The Son of God that from his enemies he may hide
The Creator who in reality needed no place to hide
For he owns all things
For "The earth is the LORD'S, and the fullness thereof,"
      [15] (The Holy Bible, Psalm 24:1 KJV, 1979).
But eye cannot see, nor ear understand
That the Creator, in your land would hide
You would offer refugee for your Lord
That in lives He may dwell
Subsequently, that peace you may finally have too.

Why should you treat my people with contempt?
Why should you degrade your fellow man?
Making him look like an animal
Yet, even a pet you keep at home is well taken care of!
An animal created lower than man
Treated well and highly regarded!

The enemy's antidote for my pain is repugnant to me
It is one made to wreck further havoc to my people
than to bring healing.
What sin have I committed against my enemy
that I may make amends?
What sin have I committed that he may accept my
    sacrifice?
I have been compliant to all his pseudo prescriptions.
But healing is still elusive.

Structural Adjustment Programme (SAP) is nothing
but a drug that breeds unemployment
and plants discord among my people
A seed planted to breed lawlessness
and an uprising against leadership
Divorce of my enemy means more economic sabotage
A definite cancellation of all support
The so-called "Debt relief!"
A Debt burden and dilemma for my leaders.

No man can ever be happy when his marriage
is controlled by external forces
No justice can be present
When his house is run by outsiders
Would you stop his fury?

Charles Kapungwe

Can you contain his rage?
Surely one day he shall rise up
To give vengeance against the wrongs
Putting an end to his troubled home.

Can my technocrats solve my fixed exchange rates?
Can they undo the fallacy
of unjust manipulation of my currency by my enemy?
Would they propose or echo Martin Luther King's
peaceful protest and demonstration,
accept Mandela's initiative
or would they take it as the
ANC's "Umkhonto we Sizwe?"
Which way mother Africa?

Is the voice of reason enough?
Can boycotting of the enemy's services pay any
        dividends?
Is civil disobedience key to freedom?
Would taking a leaf at the Montgomery bus boycott
a good strategy?
Take a lesson from your past history.
Did all your nationalists use all these means
which were at their disposal?
Is an armed struggle an answer?
Please help me reason through my clouded mind!

My enemy pleads innocent to the slain
To millions who now wallow in poverty
A case he alludes to my incapability and
        mismanagement
He is ashamed to accept that he sponsors revolt,

finances disobedience and aids insurgencies
To take over my inheritance
Why is my trade with you imbalanced?
Why should my mother pay more for your goods
and you pay less for hers?

Haiti, a product of fate and conspiracy
A story never to be shared
A story never to tell
A mortgaged nation
Debt never to repay in one's lifetime
Not even the descendants would
For yours is a nation under a lifetime mortgage
A French dynasty initiative
A scheme for Haiti millions in gold, to the master Haiti
    to give!
That "freedom" the French may grant to the "poor"
    nation
A fate and conspiracy never to announce
For shameful is the tale
That the oppressed to the oppressor they may pay
And then "freedom" to win!

"Poor quality!" you say?
Or did I not hear you well?
Is my gold of poor quality?
Is my diamond cheap?
Is my petroleum second class?
Take me to school that I may understand
this kind of scale that my enemy uses!

Take account of your uranium Namibia, Congo DR,
    Niger
Take stock of your petroleum Nigeria, Libya, Angola,
    Sudan
How about your copper, emeralds
and cobalt you Zambia and Congo DR
What is happening to your diamonds and gold,
South Africa, Congo DR, Botswana, Sierra Leone,
Ghana, Liberia?
O take stock of your minerals mother Africa!

Unless you learned what to do
with your natural resources mother Africa
someone will continue to exploit you.
Learn how to make your own products
From your gold, silver, diamonds,
copper, cobalt, uranium.
Someone will continue to reap from where he did not sow
This has just been delayed but never can it be stopped.

A United States of Africa!
A threat to the world!
The richest continent!
The most self-sufficient continent!
Where anything can grow naturally!
The largest country!
The greatest manpower!
Abundant, undepleted resources!
A great superpower!
Africa the Great!
The enemy's pain!
What hatred to see it come to pass!

Yes, for we shall overcome someday!

What should I give as appeasement to him?
What should I offer to end this calamity?
Should I give him my virgin daughters?
Should I give him my sons to do forced labour for him?
What sacrifice should his gods accept?
To end my unwarranted and continuous enslavement?

But I have done all to appease him!
He is unrelenting in his unquenchable appetite for my
      wealth
He cares less for my survival
'Till in sorrow I go to the grave
While he stares in laughter
And my children stand perplexed
that mortal man could harbour such evil and hate.

Would you accept my sacrifice?
Will you let me have a breathing space?
Won't you let me live in peace?
What wrong did I do to you
to deserve this punishment?
What is the cost for my freedom?
The price for my freedom.

History tells me tyrannies never last
Strong kingdoms never live forever
Because above lies the Almighty
Who watches and laughs
At the craftiness and intents of men
The Jews have a story to tell

Africans have theirs too
Objects of wrath by their fellow man they have been
Mortal man whose life is but a fleeting breath.
Ask Pharaoh, he will tell you
For Egypt has a story too!

What is the ransom that I may pay?
That word may go from north to south
And from east to west
To my sons and daughters
That they may work tirelessly
To purchase their freedom
And remove the shame from their face, forever
Which they have known
Since time immemorial.

That once again
They may walk as a people
With heads tall and high.
But would my enemy allow that to happen?
So, let it be O Africa!
Hope unquenched
Faith unabated.

Because someone understands, we have hope
Because He listens to the cry of the oppressed,
we have faith
Because he is close to the broken-hearted,
we have joy.
We may look weary
But our spirits are strong
No amount of hatred, oppression and injustice

can break our spirits.

I have known no strong people like you
O mother Africa!
Your sons and daughters are blessed lot
Your women are as tough as a bear
Your men as strong as a lion
Your resilience boggles your tormentors!
Your strength amazes your oppressors.

"How can a people survive on so little?" they ask
It is a sign of your unbroken spirit
Endowed on you by your Creator
A symbol of our unfailing endurance
Characteristic in the oppressed peoples of the world
Whose constant cry cannot be ignored forever
By He who listens to the cry of the oppressed
For He shall not continue to keep silent
In judgment, He shall surely arise
And all the rich shall cry!
As justice shall be pronounced, on the surface of the
        earth
And the proud shall be humbled!

CHAPTER 6
IT IS A CONSPIRACY OF DOMINATION AND POSSESSION!

It is a conspiracy,
By the "Group of 7" (8), and back to 7!
A Group of 20,
They lie in wait
To swallow up my children
Eating them alive,
Dying a slow excruciating death
With no remorse, they watch
Amidst a new ploy
To curtail me from my inheritance.

My cry is overheard across the nations
A new remedy they bring,
"Privatization," they say
Would certainly cure your ills, –
A technical term synonymous with
"Give us your wealth!"
My economists say, "Comply!"
My educationalists say,
"It is the key to high productivity!"

My leaders ignorantly sign
Selling their land but they know it not

Job losses follow, crime escalates
So, do other vices
which become the order of the day.
Like in the past,
he grins with approval
Another headache for me.

Words truly come to my memory,
Words passed on to me by my uncle,
Words uttered by the retreating enemy
As her independence Zambia finally gained;
Words of ridicule,
As he finally gave up my land
To go back to his land
Ending a bitter confrontation with mother Africa's
        nationalists
"Africa is your land," they had said,
"But the minerals are ours!" [16] (Jameson Chitonga, 1979).
A saying they were determined to see come to pass
While to sleep my mother went.

Sorrow and desperation greet my people
As the bogus investor strips, away all assets
of my once giant mines!
He retreats home after a massive externalization of
        funds.
My mines are left as white elephants!
Once the pride of the Copperbelt towns of Zambia!
My towns are now dubbed "ghost towns!"
My daughter cries foul!
"The wheels of capitalism are driven by blood," [17] (Emily
        Sikazwe, 2002)

so, says Emily Sikazwe,
A voice for the voiceless majority who stands exploited.

A briefcase company did not do the deception,
Nor was the culprit a non-reputable company
That you may accuse me of short-sightedness.
In my dealings with my oppressors
You pressurized me to privatize.
The giant corporate company Anglo-American
    Corporation
That you know well enough
Did the "rip-off!"
Leaving me in shambles
Aware that they were not obligated to pay exit costs
In breach of contract and a foreknown factor
Which President Levy Mwanawasa warns
all African leaders to be aware of! [18] (Levy Mwanawasa,
    June 2002).

The solution to my ailment
Has been endless liquidation!
Liquidate this, liquidate that!
Liquidate all viable companies that offer competition
to his industry!
Exit Zambia Airways, enter enemies' flights
Die Copperbelt Bottlers
(Manufacturers of a local Tip Top drink)
Enter Coca Cola Bottlers!
Forward with private bus companies
Goodbye United Bus Company of Zambia, (UBZ)
(A state enterprise),
Welcome Copperbelt Energy and other new mines!

Charles Kapungwe

Away with Zambia Consolidated Copper Mines,
      (ZCCM)!
(A state led major share holding company).

A deliberate ploy to annihilate my economy
Eliminating potential challengers
And make me continuously dependent
upon his resources:
The injustice of the rich who lack compassion
Delinquents, selfish, and brutal men
Doing everything at their disposal
To rule and control "their" world
An illusion that Africa now stands to challenge.

I heard my young sons cry at my ignorance,
My lack of understanding of "free market economy!"
"Nationalization was bad, mother!" they say.
"The profit margins were not sustainable!" they tell me.
"You are right sons!" I tell them.
If only you owned some of these companies
I would be a happier mother!
Alas! All you have, you have to give away!

You have deflated our ego,
You have ruined our prospects,
You have hit us on every side,
Discouragement has been your aim
To make us a powerless people;
A people full of discontentment, complaints, and
      disillusionment
Striking an arrow of death
Into every son and daughter of Africa.

Why fight a people who mean well?
Why make them objects of your wrath?
A great, peaceful and loving people,
As harmless as an ant;
And as innocent as a dove.
So, is mother Africa's offspring
who offers an olive branch to all her adversaries,
But they refuse to take it, –
Preferring to harm an innocent people.

Tears have been my food all night long
My bed is wet, drenched with tears
My eyes cannot see sleep,
We have been disgraced,
We have been oppressed,
We have been humiliated
But we still have hope!
Because our future is secure
It is not in man's hands
No, not in the donor communities' hands
But in the Great One of Israel.

Another of my sons is in a dilemma
Negotiation at the table of the enemy yielded no fruit
To the bush he took
Years of guerrilla warfare finally paid-off
Independence granted reluctantly, too late!
1980 Year of rejoicing
Zimbabwe was born!
After years of bitter confrontation with the enemy
Very fierce was the battle
The forests claimed more lives than the barrel of the gun.

His victory, however, is short-lived
As he finally discovers
What my other sons discovered earlier
They lay in wait to strangle his economy
And choke my children to death
'Till they repented of the evil of asking for liberation.
Within 20 years,
One of Africa's well-developed land
and economy now lay in ruins!
Like the ruins of the Great Zimbabwe!
A successful assault at his ingenuity and stubbornness:
Failure to comply to the rules of the game
As played from London and Washington!

Independence is no independence
When 70% majority of your people
live on 30% arid land of your country
when 30% minority in your land
live on 70% fertile land!
He questions the logic in this unfairness in distribution
    of land!
Answers cannot be found!

Like in the past the negotiating table refuses to give
    solutions
Violence ensures: a cry for equal opportunity!
Advocates and proponents of human rights go to sleep
"Like an ostrich, their heads remain buried in sand!"
Pretending they have seen nothing
Yet their media carries daily reports
Of "his view."

A 20-year renegotiating on land lapses
Someone fails to honour the promise!
The promise of redistributing land
to the displaced indigenous population
and with compensation to minority land owners
    supposedly
meant to come from the former masters
as enacted in a document in Lancaster, UK
which paved way for Zimbabwe's independence
to the now displaced land owners, fails!
But because it is one with the greater muscle
who fails to honour the promise,
No accusing finger is pointed at her!
Again, only my child is perceived to be evil
And like always is demonized!
Sanctions! Sanctions! Sanctions, he suffers!

My enemies thought 20 years were far away!
They were expecting to see a new leader.
A leader they would hoodwink,
dribble, and deceive!
But Robert Mugabe is here to stay!
A leader who had been a signatory to power transfer
to give Zimbabwe her independence in 1980,
And to forego Southern Rhodesia!
A clause on land issue is deferred!

After 20 years, Britain was set to compensate the white
    farmers!
And portions of "their" land to Africans she was to give!
So, stated their lying paper!

For 70% of arable land was in the hands of the rich
  minority!
And 30% of unproductive land was in the hands of the
  poor black majority!
So, Mugabe reminds the powers that be,
of his responsibility,
for a fair land distribution to his people,
20 years later!
In line with what their lying document had stated!
Yet not depriving others what rightly was theirs!
Only asking for justice to prevail!

You have pressed a wrong button my son!
Now they are speaking of strangulating you!
For it is good for your people to suffer!
"Do not touch us!"
"A bad leader" now you are!
"A dictator" now they say you are!
Familiar words he uses to depose of leaders!
Leaders who refuse to dance to his tune.
The same man Britain had honoured
before the issue he had raised!
"Credit freeze, assets' freeze on Zimbabwe!" says the U.S.!
Britain not to mention!
Is all they say you have asked for!
If Africa and the rest of the world were to say to them
"Sanctions, sanctions," for the atrocities
which have been committed against them,
everyone would be in bewilderment today!

It is an "international" gimmick
A worldwide ploy

To manipulate, control, and intimidate
A witchcraft type of spirit
He makes his presence felt everywhere
To carry out his ideology
An ideology of superiority complex
But mother Africa has received the greatest blow
A target of evil manipulation
Meant to paralyse her backbone.
2019, Africa mourns the death of another of its senior
statesmen!
Robert, we mourn you!

Her children are treated as aliens
In the enemy's land
Targets of police brutality
While my enemy lives superfluously in my land.
My wealth built his mansions
So, did my labour
But why do you treat me with contempt?
Why do you treat me like a second-class citizen?
Didn't you know that under my hyperpigmented skin
lies the same veins and arteries?
And a loving heart
That pumps the same red viscous fluid
A universal fluid for all mankind
For men we all are!

CHAPTER 7
SOMEONE ELSE'S HAND IS IN CONTROL OF AFRICA'S FUTURE AND DESTINY!

Africa's far-fetched dream of a utopia world
Lies at the mercy of her tormentors.
Her destiny is shaped by a few selfish world dictators
Who prey on the helpless and the disadvantaged!
None of them is ashamed that behind their high
    standard of living
lies the sweat and suffering of the voiceless majority.
Devaluation is the necessary evil of the African economy
A condition unavoidable
While my enemy's currency remains over-valued for years
A deliberate ploy against Africa.

Your quest for riches and independence is doomed
Because near you, lives your enemy
who holds a vendetta against you
Giving you a plastic smile
His offer of help not genuine.
Would you trust his remedy?
Would you accept his solutions for your ailing economy?
Would you incorporate and accept his advice?
It is a time bomb for you and your children
One meant to throw you into further misery.

Your genuine friend has been undermined
Your longstanding partner and ally has gone!
She gave you help unconditionally,
She helped you to be freed from years of unbearable
    colonialists.
She helped Angola, your son, defend her independence;
She helped your liberation movements.

African National Congress (ANC) of South Africa,
FRELIMO of Mozambique,
Zimbabwe African People's Union, (ZAPU)
United National Independence Party (UNIP).
of Zambia and Kenneth Kaunda
But now she is one of the G8!
(Now dismissed from the Group for presumed war-
    mongering!)
A fault not of her own-making
Because she did not acknowledge God in her strength
A lesson to be learned, and down she went!

Alas! Her romance with the G7 has been brief!
She is found wanting and shown the door!
Her militarism a case to fault her!
The same they too have practiced!
Yet no wrong they have seen in their adventures!
And Africa never ceases to be amazed!

Would she now re-join her tormentors and yours?
No, she would not!
A genuine friend she has been,
who trained all your men and women
Engineers, pilots, doctors, nurses, agriculturists

and of course, freedom fighters!

I bemoan your state of affairs
O mother of great riches
The ruins of your economies
Like Timbuktu, they lie in disarray,
The work of your enemy
Like the Great Zimbabwe in ruins they lie
Who shall pick up the remains?
The crumbles of your name
That you may perpetuate a legacy
For mother Africa
"That there lived a people, beautiful and humble.
Strong and caring.
A great people from the land of Africa."

Your village life mystifies your visitor,
A life lived with Mother Nature.
No worry or depression is mentioned among you
A life lived communally
Strong cords of love holding you together
No fear for the gun by day or night
No suicide bomber, rapist or child kidnapper is lurking
No child molester is a threat among you!
No drug addict is a threat among you either!
For to sleep you go daily like a baby!
Because no nuclear holocaust is ever near you
Your peace inconceivable!

Your own credentials you are made to doubt
which your own institutions offer
Ranking among the best they are

Your bright sons and daughters
With their contemporaries, abroad cannot be matched
For their education, sound it is
And so are their minds
But misplaced faith has cheered the vanquished
And downgraded the downtrodden!

When your scientists make it
Or a breakthrough looms their way
Your sons and daughters from your own womb
Indoctrinated by your enemy
"That nothing good could come out of Africa,"
tear them down!
No support is rendered
Left to be hijacked by their powerful and strong
        competitor
Pioneering work hijacked
Your scientific exploits a shadow they remain
A poignant story you carry
Credit sold to your master
Dr. Percy Lavon Julian – A life and journey fully lived
Mankind to help but powers that be
His life unappreciated and unrecognized!

Percy Julian a story of mixed fortune,
Percy Julian a story of pain and triumph;
A mind subjected to torture and difficulty,
Yet to the top it rises
To compete with his white friends in school he is
        subjected
Double classes made to cover junior and senior classes at
        a go

That as a black person to the level of his white
    counterparts to reach
To eat or sleep with the rest in dorms denied
Yet on top of his chemistry class in 1920 he came out!

A master's degree to pursue
Opportunities too narrow too few to find,
Yet against all odds a determined spirit a way for him it
    makes
Few science students, few chemistry students among his
    race to see
Kept bottled up by a systematic deliberate intent to
    segregate
A person judged by the colour of his skin
and not the content of his character[10] (Dr. Martin
    Luther King, Jr. "I have a dream," 1963).
Unmoved and undaunted by fellow man's discourse
A conscience of a people unmoved
Aimed at taming and eliminating fellow man's
    innovation and mind power
But Percy, to emancipate himself from society's injustice
and induced suffering by design he desired
To educate himself to the PhD in chemistry he chose
A course few people of African descent undertaken
in a segregated country of his!

Harvard says no!
Doctoral studies in the U.S. to a black person not be given!
His dream quashed!
But where there is a will, there is a way!
A knock at the door of Harvard finally opens!
Three years of school there, but to work not!

A top-notch student denied a piece of paper
that a doctor of chemistry he was not to be!
Only a "master" he could be!
But a doctor indeed he was, yet, a paper signed by the elite
he never was to be given!
In spite of all his years of hard work!

A teacher he was to be!
Not to compete with the establishment
For an insult to them it was!
Then to Austria he went
There to live, study and work
With top-notch scientists, he mingled!
A workaholic of a man he was
A genius among his peers never seen before!

Then to his native country, a doctor he returned
A genius in his field he was!
But in spite of his unequalled accomplishment
Another superior race he could not teach
Top schools said "no!"
Howard says "yes!"
A leading researcher, scientist he was destined to be
He disapproved the learned and corrected the superior
Inventions and patents unequalled!
A genius of geniuses
But unrecognized he remained!

Physostigmine, progesterone and testosterone
        contribution!
Cortisol contribution not to forget!

Food, chemicals, paints, an endless chain of discoveries
    under his sleeve!
But America was still not ready for a black accomplished
    chemist to be recognized!
"Nobel price material" his work was
the learned colleagues sigh!
But who said those who confer degrees
on the learned were colour blind?
Those who seek to educate masses know no race to
    favour?
But Percy, a place to live in is denied
And so are accolades from powers that be!

A place to live in by his doctor-wife and himself in Chicago's
affluent suburb comes under a test!
Fire is set to his house!
A bomb thrown at his home!
For no doctor of colour was welcome among the affluent
    and deserving!
Injustice he set to fight
That justice his people they may receive
A forgotten genius of our time
His contributions to medicine
A story never told!
But Africa remembers!

Let your sons and daughters carry out research
Let them exploit the Jungle
That on the African herbs they may conquer
Mother Nature so rich and self-sufficient
That she may give back to you healing
and beauty lotions

Your smile unfading.

Black Farmers in the U.S.A., even today (2019)
are not spared from Institutional Racism!
Huge farms inherited from grandparents and parents are
systematically being syphoned from descendants of slaves!
At one time they made up 14 percent of American
     farmers:
2 percent, now they are!
A threat from Black Farmers who at one time were
     cultivating 1,500 acres and above,
a truth someone didn't like!
In 2016, the average sugar cane farm in Louisiana was
     870 acres
One African American family once farmed up to 5,000
     acres
Nevertheless, large Black farms, are now systematically
     being wiped out
through race bating from overwhelmingly white farm
     communities and Agricultural Institutions!

Negative stereotypes meant to ensure that lenders deny
     them loans
Are ways utilised – means that ensure that a nail finally
     is being put in their coffin!
A coffin made by their enemies!

Pigford Lawsuit (Pigford v. Glickman), a huge class
     lawsuit by Black Farmers
Causes the U.S. Department of Agriculture to admit to
     discrimination on the basis of race by limiting and
     delaying Black farmers access to loans!

Following this largest settlement case in the U.S.
    government history,
USDA ultimately admits to discriminatory practices
    within its agency! [19] (NBC Left Field, 2019).

Farms being confiscated, homes on farms being
    foreclosed on.
In the "Land of the Free and the Brave"
Where I am repeatedly told "I am lazy and I don't work
    as hard as my white counterpart!"
Discrimination from Banks, USDA
"Defective soy bean sold to Black farmers!"
"Fake seeds," delivered to my people!
Sold to them by a leading multibillion-dollar seed
    company in the world
Leading to a lawsuit against the company.

Sugar Mills refused to honour contracts
to harvest sugar cane: on purpose!
Black Farms' sugar cane!
Refusing to service Black-owned farms – race a factor at
    the heart of it all
Louisiana we cry! Jim Crow Laws,
state and local laws which upheld racial segregation in
    the late 19th and early 20th centuries still causing
    my children to suffer! Even today!
Decades after their abolition!

Why let corruption eat you like a moth
Why accept a bribe from your enemy?
Selling your property and land at give-away prices
Land given away to bury nuclear waste

Other non-nuclear trash (including plastic) not to
    mention
Kickbacks accepted, your people to kill
And you know it not!
Property given at will
O ye African leaders!
Exchanging your inheritance with perishable things
Consequently, enslaving your people
And servants of your master you let them forever be.

It is the futility of humanity
An agony of destiny
Prying itself upon the unsuspecting
Yet myopic are your Presidents
Their blindness, the enemy's joy
A weakness he exploits to deceive your leaders
With kickbacks, money is rolled into their personal
    accounts
Their countries they sell.
Nuclear waste they accept to be dumped into their
    countries
Your clean land now contaminated with nuclear waste
    forever!
Cancer-causing agents you are made "to buy"
"Imported" via deceit, corruption and through a ploy to
    kill you
But you know it not!

Should mother Africa keep silent
when her enemies team up against her?
Should she watch helplessly when her children remain
    tortured

And her leaders' legs are pulled day and night?
They know not how to make bold and independent
    decisions
All her policies are but imposed instructions
Masterminded by her seemingly powerful enemy.

They tell you always what to do!
How to fix your economy,
How to run the country,
But you cannot tell them how to run theirs!
Nor would you instruct them on any major policy of
    their nations!
A paradox of modern civilisation, independence, and
    partnership!
Any resistance to any advice is deemed as undemocratic
and uncooperative
A factor serious enough to call for sanctions against you!

Would you listen if Africa told you
which leader is fit for your nation?
Would you bend if pressure were applied on you
until your policy you changed?
Would you accept an outside force to fund a political
    party?
Stop the hypocrisy and let Africa be independent!

Perhaps a lie this cry you think is!
Perhaps an Anti-West overblown out of proportion
you think this discourse is
then, think again!
Turkey is told by Trump,
"I am fully prepared to swiftly destroy Turkeys' economy

if Turkish leaders continue to go down this dangerous
and destructive path,"[20] AP, Robert Burns.
If you doubt their hand on Mother Africa, reconsider
    your stance!
Who do you think destroyed Zimbabwe?
Who destroys African countries?

Their medical personnel are free to practice
In your land without being registered!
For from afar they come
Carrying for you drugs untested by your scientists
Yet there, yours cannot!
Always perplexed are your children!

When a piece of stick you look to see in your friend's eye
A log you fail to see in your own eye
A hypocritical liar you become.
"You fool!"
First remove your log in your eye
And then go remove that which is in your friend's eye!

"Even an ant, when persistently pestered can bite,"
my mother taught me.
She said Africa shall surely awake
She shall not continuously be on the receiving end
of her tormentors, forever.
The enemy would one day be on the receiving end
awakened to his rude shock
As Africa's patience shall run out
In rage, her sons and daughters
Shall in unison proclaim:
"Enough!"

And enough it shall be!

O the pain of being ostracized!
The pain of being ignored!
An extended hand of friendship is disregarded,
For African it is!
I am taken aback –
A cold hand of friendship
Snubbed and hated for my condition
Spearheaded by a strong vendetta
of years of misinformation, exaggeration,
and stereotyping of my status!

A cruel world of discrimination it has been.
A wrong perception of Africa
makes an echo all over the world
Thanks to the successful propaganda
That my enemy has waged
Who has placed a tag on me
A label of rebel and stigmatisation!

My learned people would tell me
It is "imbalance of payments!"
It is "poor expected earnings."
"Low production is eating us up!"
But little do they see the manipulation by an external
        enemy
And wicked schemes
That fix my exchange rate
Manipulation of my currency.

6,000 to $1

10,000 to $1
is my exchange rate!
One to one never to be!
Where he has no control my exchange rate is unreasonable
Where he has control, it is reasonable!
At independence, my child's currency (Zambia) was K1
        to $2
46 years after independence
K5,000 to $1!
"An imbalance of trade" or a scheme of intent?

Implications not to tell!
To buy his currency
that to his country you may go,
through the nose you have to pay!
Your economies at ransom they are held!
To buy your currency
that to you Mother Africa they may come,
"A Merry Christmas" it is for them!
And a superfluous living in your land
They will live!
A fortune of your lifetime
to give away for you!

"Why aren't all currencies of the world be convertible
at one to one?" my daughter asks.
"Why couldn't all nations pay the same
for goods purchased from other nations,
I mean rated the same?" she inquires.
"Why does the buyer always set the price for your
        (African) goods?"
she questions.

Innocent children die.
Their mothers cry.
The sight of their offspring, a painful sight.
Ever watched a product of your womb wrinkle in pain?
Ever seen him look into your face?
Ever fathomed what he was asking you to do for him?
Would you stand that sight?
Stop it you heartless and perverse people!

Let it not be proclaimed on Mt. Kilimanjaro
Let it not be mentioned on the Alps Mountains
Let no one announce it over the Drakensberg
     Mountains
Let no one say it on Muchinga Escarpment
And on Cairo Road let no cry be heard
Lest your enemy hears of it and rejoices over you
Your struggle in food-acquisition
Your failure to feed your offspring
And your strangled economies, mother Africa
Land of my ancestry.

I bemoan your wrath
Sent by your enemies
Who work tirelessly against you
Stripping off your assets
And siphoning your wealth
Externalizing profits at an alarming rate –
Caring little
Rejoicing that both the leaders and masses in deep sleep
     they lie
Their disorganization, a point of weakness
An opportunity for his comfort

Your distress his joy.

Who shall halt this cruel trend?
That deprives natives of their inheritance
In broad daylight.
An alliance of evil-hearted men
That deprives the poor of their wealth
Leaving your blessed rich land desolate
A pleasant sight to your tormentors.

Our legs are pulled
We always dance to someone's music
He forces us to dance that his crumbs we may eat.
Dancing to his tune
Whenever our dance displeases him
He orders us to dance more vigorously
"Harder!" he says
Then ration follows
"No dance, no food:
Dancing to someone's tune," [21] (Nevers Mumba).

Because of the inequalities, disproportions, and
        stigmatisation
My children would want to obtain papers
from my enemy's place for recognition and status
How foolish!
Few of my children know and realize
that their education system
that is tailored to make them go through the mill is
        second to none
For because of your skin
To compete favourably,

twice should be your capabilities than your
    contemporaries.

None of my children has been known to fail
In the so-called "civilized world"
Provided they are not overtaken by the folly
and disintegration of life prevalent in his society
Moral erosion, insensitivity, self-centeredness
And living indulgencies and orgies in some cases.
For your children excel
and true representatives of you they are!

Someone lied to you that "it was genetic!"
"In your colour lay your problem," he said.
"To be a servant is what you were created for," said
    another
"Surely something was wrong with your constituents,"
    they claimed
But your anatomical and physiological composition
is no different!
Nor is your biochemical structure!
For this reason, you have excelled beyond their set limits.

Who shall determine for you what you can
and what you cannot do?
Who shall set limits for you?
Where you would go and where not to?
For the God-given potential in you is great
So high you cannot go over it
So wide you cannot go around it
So deep you cannot go under it
So great and huge your potential indeed is!

We are made to push enormously large stones uphill
While they push theirs downhill
The results are devastating
Casualties among my people uncountable
Perspiration covers their faces
Sweat drenches their bodies
As they attempt to roll multiple stones uphill.

Each successful attempt is greeted with a new stone to push
Days go into weeks
Weeks into months
And months into years
That new stones they may push
New conditions attached
For disposal of these death-causing stones
A pleasing aroma to my enemy
A daunting task for Africa
After all it is his game for his survival!
Played on unequal terms with his opponents.

You cushion off your enemy
Your labour feeds his children
That in luxury they may live
He preys on your energy
His economy sustained
As in jittery he stands
About your quest for equal opportunity
Being surpassed, his fear
As doom he sees for him around the corner
Should the provider of all raw materials cease to be!

Was Nelson Mandela a terrorist?

I am forced to ask!
Was Samora Machel a terrorist?
Were Jomo Kenyatta, Kenneth Kaunda,
Augustino Neto, Sam Nujoma, Kwame Nkrumah,
Joshua Nkomo, Robert Mugabe terrorists?
Was Martin Luther King, Jr. a terrorist?
To you they were
To me freedom fighters they are
Heroes of the silent oppressed majority
Liberators of the voiceless.

When they go to war, their slumped economies pick up!
When my children and I go to war, our economies
        slump!
A paradox of fate
So, to war they shall constantly ever go
That well to them it may be
But alas to you all to whom woes should never depart!
Who can count the number of the casualties?
For numbers and statistics, you are
Human beings; – super humans, others are,
So, going to war is their delight!
And warmongers they are!

My quest for equality is perceived as a threat
A danger to his national security so, they say
My quest for fair treatment is misinterpreted and
        misunderstood
Viewed with enormous suspicion
Luther is charged with "Disturbing the peace!"
Mandela is charged with treason!
But equal opportunity is my cry

Equal opportunity in education
Equal opportunity in health and trade
Provision of social justice, political independence, and
      fair play.

Africa seemingly faces a tough nut to crack
As all odds appear to be against her
A difficult mountain to climb
A deep valley to pass
And a wide river to cross
But there is no high a mountain, no deep a valley
And no wide a river that cannot be crossed
Your intuition, courage, and strength will guide you
For surmounting every hurdle, you shall that lies in your
      path.

Your enemy will be dismayed
At your endurance, he shall fume
Your lack of discouragement will appal him
As you lead your children to heights unreached
Like an eagle you will soar high
The storms you shall squarely face
And up you shall be lifted
For your Creator will fight for you
For, "The race is not to the swift
or the battle to the strong," [22] (Ecclesiastes 9:11, NIV).

Unaware of the injustices of their nations
their political machinery has created
are many sincere citizens
As they graduate from the quiet life of society

Soon they are assimilated into the old game of extortion
    against Africa
Soon innocent citizens become a part of a
worldwide web of strangulation of Africa.

Genuine citizens are concerned about the plight of Africa
Many at G8 (G7) or G20 meetings, gather with the
    afflicted to protest
But alas!
For few they are!
Would they lobby against their governments?
Would their voices be combined with the African voice
against their nations?
Would their reasoning fall on deaf ears?
Would they say, "Because of our injustices
we have prospered?"
Would they say, "Because of our craftiness
we have prospered?"
Siphoning wealth from the unsuspecting
and manipulating the exchange rate to our advantage
and to the disadvantage of Africans!

Gaining profits and interests from extortion
Interest rates that skyrocket uncontrollably high
and out of reach of even any cooperating and yielding
    nation
to our ever changing and amended conditions!
No government would meet!
Enclosures of hypocrisy
That we call "Business principles and clauses!"
"International credit cards" which prey on borrowers
Debts never to be repaid in our lifetime

or that of our children's children!

IMF, World Banks, World Trading Organisation
(WTO), Bloomberg, Rating Agents: (Moody),
Standard & Poor (S & P), all U.S. – based!

They speak the same language and are supported by
their stooge!

Rating Agents who are coerced to change credit ratings
of our countries, via speculations at any time!

And interest rates immediately go up!

Would the pressure groups at home join the voice of
reason?

Would they say,

"It is immoral to have our currency stable

for decades at the expense of Africa?"

For theirs we have kept in three to four digits or more

against ours which we ensure remains only one digit!

"Since Africa's real enemy is *US*!"

If they don't say it,

Africa shall say it!

Africa shall rise up against tyrants

who have contributed to social upheavals in her society

Africa shall resist evil

Africa shall oppose all crookedness

and enslavement and free herself!

For Africa shall with a shout cry out

In unison, she shall shout:

"Let freedom ring"[10] on the Alps Mountains

(Martin Luther King, Jr., "I have a dream," 1963,
paraphrased).

Let freedom ring on Drakensberg Mountains

Let freedom ring on Mt. Kilimanjaro
Let freedom ring on the territories of Guinea Bissau!"

CHAPTER 8

YOUR LEADERS, SOMETIMES A LET DOWN THEY HAVE BEEN!

Your leaders, sometimes
a shame they have been!
They are men without insight and understanding
Blinded from real issues which afflict and pester mother
    Africa
To the enemy they have looked for survival
To the wind they have thrown their dignity
Like sheep and goats needing a shepherd
they have been!

A shepherd from the West to come
That a way they may be shown
For in the thicket and maze of mediocrity
they have wandered
Led by the same shepherd they look to for salvation.

Your leaders, a shame they have been!
Lured by the enemy
Your wealth worth billions of dollars they have deposited
Into Swiss and other foreign accounts
Mobutu Sese Seko
Sani Abacha
President Obiang Nguema

Jean-Pierre Bemba
Joseph Kabila.
War-related crimes not to mention!
Blaise Compaoré,
Charles Taylor,
Gnassingbe Eyadema,
Africa, mourns.

So, are the rebels, Jonas Savimbi
They go the way of the earth
Leaving you with no inheritance
While the recipients grin with approval
For the African wealth, the West inherit
Mother Africa never to be given back her stolen money
Nor could it be used to cancel her
"Hypocritical foreign debt!"
Funds "locked up" in a safe you couldn't open!
Alas! Riches too wonderful to part away with!
Bloody money to keep!

Their lack of insight is a victory for the enemy
Why should corruption be synonymous with you?
O Cameroon?
Why should it be a tag for you O Nigeria?
Why should bribery be your byword O Congo DR.?
Why should mismanagement be part of you?
Why should greed rule in you?
Don't you have a feeling for your children and your
    women?

Why accept a bribe that corrupts the heart?
Practicing extortion that turns a wise man into a fool

and blinds your eyes
That justice you see not
Faithfulness and impartiality are stolen from you
Turning a blind eye to what is wrong
Covering evil and promising protection!
Subjugating justice and harming the innocent
who deserves protection!

Will the human activists release the money for you?
Will the champions for the rule of law
disclose how much the pilferers had?
Will the elites of democracy part away
with what is not rightly theirs
and honour the owners of stolen wealth – the Africans?
Would they give back that which was dubiously
    acquired?
Oh yes, they will!
"Angola, here is your money!" they would say
Congo DR come and get that which is rightly yours!
Liberia, Sierra Leone, Nigeria, Sudan, Ethiopia,
Somalia, Eritrea, Libya, an endless list!

Surely from the poor they cannot steal!
For true democracy, they seek
And for justice they demand!
And so, the once "frozen" assets
and money from your pilfering nationals
will be unfrozen!
Enough heat they have to unfreeze it!
The champions of liberty and fair play,
your wealth, they shall return!

Release of political prisoners they press for
And tolerance for opposing views they ask for
For support of faction groups has not been their
    intention
Supply of guns to them an oversight it has been!
An unintended oversight!
Now that their allies are gone
who cost Africa innumerable loss of life,
atrocities and stolen wealth
Africa shall truly be remembered
Her wealth she shall receive back!

Because they mean well
An interest to the stolen money they shall add!
For a mistake, it was
That an allowance was made
That in Swiss banks the money was deposited!
In Cayman Islands (offshore sanctuary) it was secured!
In Panama it found sanctuary!
An oversight it was
That Britain could receive it!
And undesirable it was
For Corporate America to court it!
For drug money, they accept not!
Nor do they embrace any money laundering!
"This, bloody money it had been,"
They would not touch!

"A civilized world we are," they would say
A people opposed to theft!
"For the same reason our prisons
are full of coloured boys!

For lawlessness we tolerate not!
Champions of human rights we are
And the world we shall continuously show
who we are!
For a guise, it is not
That we fight evil all over the world!
That we may protect 'this, our interests!'
Weeping and wailing we shall ensure
That they never cease outside our world
Then a peaceful home we shall have
And that we shall maintain!"

To our interest it is
To see over a million-people maimed in Angola!
Millions on crutches and wheel chairs
For we did try to make them look like those from
      Vietnam
Seniors in wheel chairs
Shipping and planting millions of landmines
in Angola and southern Africa (Zambia and Zimbabwe
      included), we regret not!
For our democracy, we export
And costly always it has been!

"Landmines against a legitimate government in Angola
We helped to plant
Though through a landslide victory
a legitimate government to the pinnacle of power in
      1975 had ascended
Against their colonial masters, the Portuguese they had
      desired
to dislodge!

For no true genuine elections are accepted by us
should a stupid people choose a leader with a different
    ideology from us!
That is 'no true democracy!'
Remember Turkey? And forget not Israel (Palestine!) Or
    Egypt!
Only when a puppet we produce
That our oppressive and manipulative system we may
    perpetuate
Then democracy has been embraced!"

So, Dr. Jonas Savimbi the villain for 26 years we
    supported
Little did we care for the dying and the crippled?
The same reason why we veto resolutions
to stop the manufacturing of these
"democracy crippling tools" called landmines!

In death Mobutu mourns!
Abandoned by those who put him and sustained
him into power
Left to rot, his money in foreign accounts "not to find!"
His henchmen told!
African leaders now he warns,
"The West not to trust!"
Used and abandoned in death
His money not see!
A confession of a fool at his deathbed!

To isolate South Africa during the era of apartheid
was not to our interest
So, sanctions we flouted!

This we did with pride
For to no one are we answerable!
But if you flout sanctions against Libya, Iraq, North
     Korea,
Your children and your women, we will rip open!
Your men will be "history"
For surely from their hidden places
we will smoke them out
and that is not partiality
for we know best how the world ought to be run
and that also is democracy at its best!

When the then one-time condemned prisoner Mandela
Visited Libya at the height of "UN" sanctions
When Libya he visited soon after his release
from the 27 years of incarceration
Vehemently we announced
that wrong it was for him to visit!
But the boy said, "Who are you to tell us
who we should befriend and who we should not?"
The boy further said,
"Where were you in times of our distress?
Who supported us in the times of our distress but Libya!"
For too cheeky he was again to further state,
"Where were the so-called humanists,
For it was Libya that supplied us support
to dislodge the enemy!"
Too smart was the boy for us
that our mouths could utter no word anymore!

Why do you despise yourself?
Why do you look down upon yourself?

Why doubt your capabilities?
Thinking low of yourself now you shall stop
And above your confines and boundaries
shall you rise.

For this we believe you shall
Why not make your own products?
Why give your minerals away at give-away prices?
Why can't you make finished products for yourself?
Yes, African cars shall soon come out of you – "Africar"
African buses shall ride your highways and byways –
    "Afrobus"
Everybody shall mount on your bikes – "AfroBikes"
Your women and men shall fly their own African planes
Genuine Air Africa!
Jumbo jet 747 "Africair"
Then to the "moon" you shall go!
From Cape Town, Rabat, Cairo, Nairobi, Abuja, Lagos,
    Algiers, Tripoli, Tunis,
Kinshasa, Addis Ababa, Accra, Lusaka!

This shall happen when the artificial boundaries
That separate you from your brother and sister
shall finally crumble
Like the Berlin Wall erected by evil men
To keep a single nation divided shall be no more
Like the demilitarized zone of Korea that divides a
    nation
Shall not be allowed to continue
The watchdog of its continued existence is a foreign
    power!
Keeping a nation not unified, divided for decades!

A constant threat to a people
A threat of a nuclear holocaust
A game they are always careful is played away from
     home!

Would you listen to the voice of reason?
Would you cease your unfair policies?
Which bring forth extortion
You continue exacting usury
To a defenceless people
Creating artificial inequalities
Which force the hapless people
To be enslaved
That to you they may perpetually return for more relief
     and aid!

Yes, my leaders, a shame sometimes they have been!
Brace for a new leadership
Empowered by a right education on issues Africa faces
and by the Spirit of the Holy One of Israel
An education that makes them a proud people
A people who never look down upon themselves anymore
A people who with an empty bowl to the West will no
     longer go
Begging for relief, that their purposely maligned
     economies
May be jumpstarted,
a fallacy and tale made to be believed
By powers that be!
But to themselves and to their God they shall go
A revelation and knowledge from on high on how to
     govern, to receive!

Like Daniel, Moses, Joseph, and David they shall be!

Medicines from Africa, for Africa, they shall synthesize
A reliance upon the West never to be
Trust eroded, our killers not to trust
Vaccines, our chemists to make
For to make their own medicines they are determined
And Africa shall indeed wake up from her slumber!
That a genocide of our people may be put to an end
        forever.

CHAPTER 9

AFRICA:
A BURDEN TOO
GREAT TO BEAR!

Why create a debt burden
That is meant to last a lifetime?
A deliberate policy to enslave my people
Your leaders' initiative to build roads, schools,
houses, and to provide medicines is hijacked.
It is turned into a trap to woo them into
unending loans that will last a lifetime
A carefully planned venture to yoke my children forever.
Developed countries' interest rates are 3% on loans or less!
Developing countries' interest rates 10 to 15% on loans!
(Non-IMF loans, i.e., short-term loans, such as
    Eurobonds)
The high interest rates are not due to high risks
but are based on an overwhelming desire to milk the cow!

To "build foreign reserves in their countries"
is a wish they instigate on us!
A song synonymous to:
"Give us your gold so we would keep for you!"
Then a loan from us you qualify to get!
Meaning "Your banked wealth" will be given to you as a
    loan!
For "dull and daft you are!" so they say

Their game plan not to see!
Only your built-up foreign reserves in our land,
"collateral" we can call!
So the undiscerning cow we may milk again!

Why do you scoff at me when for alms I ask?
Why do you regard me with contempt
when you look at me?
Are you not aware of my story?
Don't you know my plight?
Didn't you know someone's ultimate wish for me?
Making me dependent
that terms may be dictated to me
Don't you know that your foundation
was erected at the cost of my sons?
My children's sweat established your very pride of today
At no cost at all yet you continue to rip off my
        continent!

I bemoan you O Africa!
Your eyes remain swollen
Like one who has known no sleep for days
Tears roll down your cheeks
They flow down like streams of your land
Not a day do they cease
They are tears not of laughter
Nor are they tears of joy
But tears of great anguish and sorrow they are
For excruciating pain, they bear
Great sorrow they harbour
And enormous anguish they court.

A $10 phone call to Africa gives you 30 minutes!
A $10 phone call to Europe gives you 5 hours!
One to Australia gives you nearly the same hours!
You wonder who is being made poor!
And Africa, the pain she bears!

A genuine friend you lack
An all-weather friend cannot be found
No, not among "them!"
Crookedness, craftiness, and cheating
lie behind offers for help
What he shall get from you in return
is the motive that moves your so-called "Cooperating
        partners."
No help rendered
No care given
No relief given
Has been given genuinely or freely
For, "Each year during the late 1990s," we are told,
"African countries paid $162 billion more than they
        received in new loans,
up from $60 billion in 1990!" [23] (Patrick Bond,
        Cultivating African Anti-Capitalism, April 2005).
"Mid-2000, U.S. Exim Bank offered $1 billion in loans
        for African countries to import anti-retroviral drugs
        to combat HIV/AIDS
$2 trillion in foreign debt in 2000 to repay,
(up from $1.3 trillion during the early 1980s)," [24]
        (Patrick Bond, 2003).

No compassion
No kindness

No empathy
Have been aroused among them
For they could have said,
"Stop the extortion!"
"Stop the usury!"
For the rip-off has been enough
Great has been our harvest
From an unsuspecting people
An open-hearted people
A humble and friendly people.

Much we have taken
Much we have stolen
Much we have grabbed
Enough, enough, enough!

An urge and appetite for blood encompass him.
No continent has been spared from my enemy's
        grandiose appetite
Indians' blood in North America spilled
In America and Canada wailings I heard!
Jews in Europe mourn!
Aborigines in Australia cry!
South America, New Zealand,
and Indians in Asia have a story to tell too.
So, has Japan
But Africa's cry surpasses them all
Over two million deaths Southern Africa to liberate [24]
(Patrick Bond, Cultivating African Anti-Capitalism,
        February 2003).
My enemy's wealth is stained with blood: African blood
Yet no shame covers his face

No remorse keeps him from wrong.

Over 500,000 killed in Angola
Murdered in cold blood
Millions permanently maimed there
As an unjust war is waged against my people
Thousands disabled by my enemy's landmines
which he refuses to be banned.
Since none of his people are victims,
but my children's children
None of his products of conception
know how to weep and wail
Since he secures his area
And allows no battles on his land
Battles seen fit only on other peoples' soil!

Jody Williams, a teacher cum activist cries
That the world may heed
The evils of land mines
Deadly weapons in wartime planted
An aftermath killer of innocent civilians
Profit-motivated killing and maiming-machines they keep
International Campaign to Ban Land Mines (ICBL) not
    to heed
1997 Nobel Peace Prize, Jody to keep
Her noble cause to reward
But shall profit-motivated nations heed the call?

"Freedom!" he cries
Yet my people still remain in bondage
In my enemy's land
Disadvantaged in everything

In the "Land of Freedom!"
It has been darkness and mist
For all my people
In the "Land of Democracy!"
Injustice and oppression
In the "Land of Liberty!"
Exploitation and inequality
In the "Land of the rule of law!"
Racial profiling and marginalization
In the "Land of equal opportunity for all!"

Prison walls are their mansions
A shelter by design.
In the land of equal opportunity!
Oh "if prison walls could talk!" [25] (Richard Wurmbrand,
      1964).
In Europe, they cry!
In Asia, they wail!
And in America they lament!
But would prison walls talk?

Would the enforcers of the law speak out
of their police brutality
against my people?
Would this unjust system be guiltless?
Would the system have a moral right
to demand for justice in distant lands?
My sons and daughters fought for justice and freedom.
They joined my enemy despite their ill-treatment at home
Fighting for "justice and freedom" for others in distant
      lands
Vietnam, Korea, and in Europe.

And Africa joined the world in World Wars
That Hitler, the fascist, they would dislodge.
But under their nose freedom and justice
an illusion it remained: a hypocritical world!

I bemoan your pain
Afflicted by your enemy, O mother Africa
You have known suffering for centuries
Your enemy committed thousands of acts
of mass murder against you
19th and 20th centuries plunder of the African continent
In the name of civilisation of the heathens
So, it was done
An insult it was.

On land and on sea they went
The way of the earth
The forests claimed many lives
And so, did the waters
Of the innocent loving souls
A sacrifice to the god of capitalism they became.

You stand stained with blood
Your hands have shed innocent blood for centuries
And your conscience pricks you not
"Innocent," so you plead
While my ancestors' blood spilled by your rifle and sword
The blood that still cries for "vengeance!"

Who can count the number of the slain
in the cotton fields or across the oceans?
Who can give the numbers of those slain in their beds

and their wives taken to their masters?
Who can count the molested young women
Falling prey to the marauding hands of their masters?
Would you say, "No" to restitution?
Would you say, "No" to affirmative action?

No amount of repayment could cover for the injustices
that Africa has suffered
No amount of restitution could cover for the evil that
Africa has known
No amount of repayment could rebate for the misdeeds
of the cruelty that Africa has experienced
Yes! But someone must gather the courage
And would say, "Africa, we are sorry!"

Stop nagging Africa
All you evil people!
Condition after condition
Proposal after proposal
Prescription after prescription
Solutions meant to haunt my mother and her children
for years.
Few of my enemy's children realize that
behind their affluence is the sweat of millions of Africa's
children
Behind my enemy's prosperity
Lies the broken backs of the poor
Driving the machinery of capitalism
Unmindful of the toil and suffering of Africa.

"Shut up! Shut up!" You say!
"Who rules your people but your people?"

"Who steals from your people but your people?"
Oh yes, ignorant you are!
Your folly cannot be hidden!
Who fixes the trade imbalance?
Who determines the price for my goods?
Who fixes the exchange rate so that it favours you and it
    disfavours me?
Did you say, "Africa you are independent?"
Or did you mean to say, "Africa you are dependent!"
Come to your senses that we may debate the issues
For unjust has been your scale
And unjust have been your policies
towards my people – Africa!

Stop the carnage
Stop the slaughter of my people
Thousands of Africans died in your quest to colonize
    Africa
Thousands died as he tried to sustain colonization
Thousands died at the hands of the Boers
to sustain apartheid
Hundreds died as you tried to sustain the Federation
of Northern Rhodesia, Southern Rhodesia and
    Nyasaland
Millions died when they resisted
to be bought or sold as goods into slavery
And thousands died during the aftermath
of a "Unilateral Declaration of Independence" (UDI)
by Ian Smith's Southern Rhodesia – Zimbabwe.

Thousands died at sea and in the cotton fields of the
    enemy

Thousands died trying to flee to freedom
Thousands died due to injustice and oppressive laws
The "Supreme Court" of the "Free World" classified
    them as "property!"
Thousands died at the hands of police brutality
Thousands died trying to set themselves free
Remember, no government has ever
granted freedom to its citizens without a fight!
Africa has and will continue to fight!

But Africa has lived with terrorists for centuries
These terrorists travel incognito
They took her women and children
The women were caressed by the enemy,
while their husbands watched helplessly
In them came children whose fathers denied fathering
    them!
But my son was heavily scolded and brutalized
if found with my enemy's daughter!
A world of discrepancy
Simon Mwansa Kapwepwe, the great African scholar
and politician writes, "Africa, we can forgive, but we
    cannot forget!"

Children of Soweto echo the anthem:
"Yes, they scare us
We are but children
We are afraid,
But we will not forget!" [26] (Sarafina – Whoopi Goldberg,
    1992).

Should Africa hit back?

Should she mobilize herself to slaughter her enemies?
Would the voice of reason permit her?
Would she declare the UN irrelevant?
Should Africa go for the jugular vein of her oppressors?
To wipe out a long living legend of an international
　　dictator?
A monster that is bent on causing havoc
Destabilizing, humiliating, and suppressing my people.

But a nation of civility you are!
A nation of hope and faith you are!
A people of peace and a large heart
who open her arms to strangers
Feeding a people from a distant land
For cruelty to humanity you refuse to abode
In you lies senescence of civility
A cradle for hope and love.

"No, no!" I heard her son say, "No!"
Payment of evil for evil is not right!
"Physical force of hate must be overcome by soul force
　　of love!"[27] (Martin Luther King, Jr., Sixteenth
　　Street Baptist Church, 1963).
No amount of hate for hate can bring about right
Since your enemy has a conscience,
To his conscience we shall speak
We shall lift no stone at no one.

"If there is something I must say to my people,
who stand on the warm threshold
which leads into the palace of justice,
in the process of gaining our rightful place,

we must not be guilty of wrongful deeds.
Let us not seek to satisfy our thirst for freedom
by drinking from the cup of bitterness and hatred."[10]
    (Martin Luther King, Jr. "I have a dream," 1963).
So, their God-sent leader they shall heed
His message, a message of the Saviour
A message which tells you that
your neighbour and enemy you must love
And this we heed!

Providentially, too, there stand a people of integrity
In the land of Africa's enemies
A people who stood against injustice
A people who helped free the slave
A people who saw the unjust system that oppressed
A hapless people
And they stood with you to condemn the injustice
That same voice is still there among many today!
And still cries out for justice!
To them Africa appreciates!
To them Africa says "Thank you!"

I heard them say,
"Sorry for the past misdeeds
Sorry for the current evil
We have treated you wrongly
We have stolen from you
We have treated you unjustly
Our riches have come by way of oppression of the weak
Our comfort has come by the way of misusing
and overusing of a people
Whose weakness we have exploited

And whose resources we have tapped."

We have made unjust laws
Laws that favour the oppressor
and disfavour the oppressed
They have had had no means to undo
our cleverly executed machinery
Because of our great wealth
We sustain operations, even far off
To plant and sponsor strife and uprisings
We have pleaded innocent
But this we have done to keep our interests going!
We are guilty indeed!
But we cannot readily admit to that!

We always wonder why many nations harbour
ill feelings and resentment towards us
"Why do they have so much hatred towards us?" we ask
"Why do they act the way they do towards us?" we
          inquire.
Yet we are not ready to listen to the truth
The real answer we choose to listen from the slanted
          opinion,
his view.
We refuse to let history say what she has to say
We once again let our interests interpret events
We are not ready to make amends!
Nor are we ready yet to say, "Please forgive us!"

CHAPTER 10
AND TO SLEEP
GOES THE
MOTHER BODY!

Defiance of the UN by any "lightweight" nation
     brought scolding
and punitive measures upon that nation
Defiance of the UN by any "heavyweight"
nation is let to pass unnoticed – like nothing ever
     happened!
The UN preaches democracy it does not practice!
It tries to enforce democracy it is guilty of violating
"Why should Africa democratize?" we ask.

When small nations rise up against other small nations
to protect themselves from hypocritical heavyweights,
the heavyweights in the name of the "UN"
or "International Community" shout:
"Sanctions! Sanctions! Sanctions!"
Like fools they hear from his master's voice
And they call it "Resolution 236 of the UN!"
But Africa knows it is the oppressors'
resolution to afflict the weak
And not of the "majority" or of the "International
     Community."
As they are erroneously dubbed!

But now the UN has lost its teeth
As the two B-s roll into Iraq unconstitutionally
The UN tacks its tail!
Shame, shame, shame!
An open humiliation, insult and a slap in the UN's face
Is not challenged with any resolution!
The duo amasses numerous Weapons of Mass Hypocrisy
    (WMH).
against a nation with no army!
A nation whose army has been disintegrated
by the so-called "UN sanctions!"
His master's voice and plan of strangulation
of a hapless and defenceless people!
Fighting and killing a people whose arms
have been tied by the "UN!"

Now the UN has become a stench to nations
Silence means consent
Shall anyone move a second motion to disarm the
    aggressor?
No! Not even one for all tails are tacked!
No, for surely, they cannot bite the finger that feeds
    them!
Nor can they bite the finger that threatens them!

As the witch goes hunting in other peoples' backyards
That fetishes they may not hide
Fetishes they have not possessed
While his, he continues to stockpile!
New technology he continues to employ
That earthlings he may rule

An unprecedented and unequalled reign of terror he
    may have
No question, no challenge he may encounter
For other witches in hiding they go
No voice, no cough is heard among them
For in great fear they are for the great witch
His gigantic eyes pop at any that dare challenge him
And in hiding go the smaller witches!

It is an impartial world
A cruel world
The world that destroys the weak
And acquits the guilty
The world that punishes the disadvantaged
And frees the oppressor
The weak is found guilty of war crimes
and is severely punished
The strong is set free: for lack of evidence!
The weak is asked to forgive and forget
and is applauded for the "Truth and Reconciliation
    Commission."
that is expected of him to have and is applauded for it
Because one of theirs is the culprit!
The strong is acquitted
They ask nations to sign a treaty
not to extradite any of their fighting personnel
for crimes committed by their nationals in war time!
What a world we live in!

Mandela is asked to forgive and forget
A Truth and Reconciliation Commission is instituted
An innocent man is incarcerated

27 solid-years of one's life
Sold to the dogs
For 26 years in the apartheid dungeons
Walter Sisulu had been!
Champions of democracy overwhelmingly,
their incarceration supported
Sanctions breached daily under their noses
And no word to speak!

For Africa, a people you are not!
A people not to care about!
"Dr. Death" is freed!
For lack of evidence!
Freed for crimes committed outside South Africa
A fairy-tale of justice!
And the UN intervenes not
Nor do the champions of democracy
Who see it as an "internal affair!"

But down goes Charles Taylor
The first former President to go
A once upon a time runaway inmate
From their jail, revenge to catch up with him!
And so, goes Bemba
While Liberia and Congo DR helplessly watch
None of your courts could ever charge
Bush for crimes against humanity
One reason why witchcraft you must not practice
All your fetishes to the "UN inspectors" to surrender!
That your errant leaders, the know-it-all would
        discipline!

Bashar Assad, Syrian President
His people he killed in a protracted civil conflict
Unlike in Libya where to the rubberstamp Mother Body
they rushed to,
Resolution too quick too swift to enact
That their African enemy quickly they may dispose of
For Syria, they could not!
In spite of "his people he killed!"
And more than the number of Libyans lay the slain!
And you still are convinced
that it was to save the people
that they had quickly rolled their killing machines into
        Libya?

Bashar Assad, Syrian President
His people he killed too!
The West's proposal to intervene militarily
But a veto from Russia and China,
a poke into witches' popping and protruding eyes!
Their readiness to mount on brooms to go and spill
        blood quashed!
Now a new offer from London and Washington
To the table of Assad, they bring
Unmindful of the law that has slain other leaders
Saddam Hussein and Muammar Gaddafi not to recall,
still in place!
Immunity the West to offer Assad so they unanimously
        agree
"If only he steps down!"
Asylum to be granted
And none in the UN reminds them of the UN mandate!

For they too know that their body is a rubberstamp of
　　the wealthy
That dances to their tune!
For to sleep it has gone!
And to bed with them it sleeps!
Double standards of justice this really is!

Why do nations plot and conspire?
Why do they conspire against the weak
and defenceless?
Why do nations rise up against those who oppose
neo-colonialism and imperialism?
Why do nations want others to be always
impoverished and in subjugation?
Why should other people's distress,
suffering, and humiliation be these nations'
joy and profit?
Why should other people's pain and sorrow
be your comfort?
Why should you let their toil
and sweat be your luxury and subsidy?
Surely destiny and posterity
will never allow this injustice to be perpetrated and
　　perpetuated
nor the disproportion to continue forever.

Why do you scoff at the displaced?
Why do you ask, "Why are they coming here?"
Have you forgotten that you have annihilated their
　　dwelling place?
Their home rich in history quashed within days!
Clandestinely destroyed or into rubble turned

Mourning never to go away
Infrastructure ruined!
Unknown to the elite that the masses to their nations
in numbers, they shall try to immigrate
Now a "global catastrophe of the immigrant problem"
they see!
Quickly forgotten are those
who had mounted on brooms to go and spill blood afar!
A dwelling place of a people to destroy!
And the simple fail to fathom
How the "learned" get muzzled and misled!

Their arsenals they cannot destroy
But neighbours' arsenals they seek
and demand destroyed
Yet even a child knows that he who has a gun in hand
A gun pointed at you is in control
Has power over you
To him you bow or he squeezes life out of you
The game your friend plays
A game he hopes always to win
for a bully you become
when an edge in your arsenals you have
over your friend.

So, this power they seek
That you may be dominated
And told what to do
A thing they enjoy to see!
Who shall bring it to an end?
That on equal footing you may all stand?
And in mutual respect you all may be!

Fighting we shall
But from a weak position you fight
No option you have
But "Peace and Reconciliation Committees" you make!
For from a weak position you fight.
When from a weak position you fight
Then "Non-violence protest" [10] you espouse (Martin
    Luther King, Jr. "I have a dream").
For from a weak position you fight
No weapon in your hand you hold.

Like Israel, none had a weapon
All the weapons were in the Philistine camp
None could they make
For the Philistines ensured none was made in Israel
That to them they may submit
A threat Israel were not to be.

A legacy adopted by my adversary
Who disarms all nations
While armed to the teeth, they remain
A philosophy few could explain
A policy too incriminating to divulge
For there too lies the cunningness and craftiness of man
Who cares less for the other
As long as his table is full
His spouse and children are well-taken care of
In this, our foreign interest!

Natural calamities we accept
Man-made ones we denounce
Natural calamities we understand

Man-made ones we condemn
Whether self-afflicted or foreign-induced
Engineered, that chaos may be the order of the day
Self-rule and rest elusive dreams to be
Busy to be kept
To fight an endless battle meant not to be won
That money and wealth into their bosoms
may forever flow
While others, disgruntled beggars
perpetually they may remain.

From the eyes of the African child come mourning
Through the lenses of the oppressed we view our world
With an unadulterated vision, we perceive
An uncorrupted worldview as interpreted by her sons
and daughters
For a slanted world opinion, they have carried
History written by the oppressor
His story has been
His story to tell
Told to cover his wrongs and roles
In a decimation and annihilation of a people
That her land, an inheritance for them it may be
While destitute and beggars Africans become
In the land of their ancestry.

Fate and a utopia world lie in our hands
Change lies in our hearts
When we come to the glimpse that we can
rise above our circumstances
when we refuse to be in defeat
when we refuse to court and entertain failure

when we disperse the lies spoken about us
when we use the God-given abilities to change ourselves
when we embrace education as our tool and hammer
that will dismantle the imaginary walls erected around
     our minds
Prison walls built by the supposedly superior race
A psychological warfare they had and still keep on
waging.
But Africa and the rest of the world through God
have crashed down the walls!

Africa salutes millions of men and women
Non-African
In the land of my enemies
Who share not with my enemy
The crooked and cruel stand of my enemy
Men and women of integrity they are
They share the grief and anguish of my people
They are the same colour as my enemy
But they refuse to carry out the machinations of my
     enemy
For they know what lies behind melanin: the human
     soul
So, at G8 (G7) meetings, protesters they mobilize
That a voice of reason "White collar" dictators would
     listen
And a sanctioned illegitimate legitimate plunder
through UN undemocratic mandate the world they may
     rule!

The human soul is not black
The human soul is not white

The human soul is not red
The human soul is not yellow
So, they believe
Behind the front that every man parades,
lies the same common basic needs of man:
shelter, food, and clothing
So, they refuse to be hypnotized
By hate-driven motives
Millions supported Martin Luther King, Jr.'s cause
Millions stood by Nelson Mandela
Millions stood by Mahatma Gandhi
And millions stood for the Jewish cause
"For all people are the same," they say.

We salute them for seeing beyond colour
We salute them for standing for a just cause
For humanity needs healing
Hate and vengeance is of the devil
Love and reconciliation is of God
Peace and tranquillity, we all seek
That justice would flow down like a river
Bringing healing and hope to broken souls
and the world would be a better place.

Will you join these millions,
you enemy of mine?
Will you see me as your partner?
Will you share with me your goods
and I will share mine with you?
Shall we accept each other's differences
as the power of diversity?
Shall we agree to complement each other's

weaknesses and strengths to better ourselves?
Shall we stop belittling one another?
Surely savages we are not
And animals we are not
But human beings who share same
and similar emotions and needs we are!

Africa, mother Africa!
Land of the strong and mighty!
A place where our ancestors trod
A place where they roamed the jungles and forests
Hunting the impala and the kudu for food
Slaying the rhino and the elephant for meat,
The tasty game meat
Your rich land yields a thousand crops
So, abundant is your rainfall
That falls "unapologetically."
Watering your land of abundance
Your gardens and forests
your produce they enormously yield
That you have insufficient food to feed your offspring
is an insult
That you go around with an empty bowl begging for
        food
and handouts from your enemy is salt added to injury
While the Mother Body created to administer world
        justice
is in deep sleep
and her snoring signalling not to be disturbed!

CHAPTER 11

A PLACE ENDOWED WITH GREAT MINERAL WEALTH!

Africa, mother Africa
Land of the energetic and the great
A place where my fathers toiled
A place where thousands upon thousands of my people
    trekked
From the village to growing towns they trekked
In search of employment they came
And none was turned away
For your giant mines swallowed all and everybody
who for employment came.

Below the surface they worked
Underground they toiled
There, they blasted the African rock
They drilled through the African rock
They burrowed through the African rock like a worm
Like a rat from above to "1340 level" (408.4 m) they went
To subvertical levels of "1390" (423.7 m) below they
    reached!
2880 to 5600 feet (877.8 to 1,706.9 meters) below the
    surface!
For over a quarter of a century,
the rock became my grandfather's,

and my father's home away from home
There in the African rock they made theirs and our living!
For mine boys, they were.

The Copperbelt Province of Zambia,
a hive of activity it became!
Zambia with a highest per capita income in
Sub-Saharan Africa (then second only to South Africa)
Konkola Mine (Chililabombwe), the world's wettest mine
brought out your copper
Nchanga Mine, Chingola (boasting then of the world's
      largest open pit mining),
yielded the ore (and so were her shafts)
Chambeshi Mines gave you her share and so did
      Kalulushi Mine
Mufulira Mine brought forth her shares too and so did
      Kitwe's
Mindolo Mine, Central, and South Orebody Shafts
      (S.O.B.) of Nkana/Kitwe
as to the world they coughed out their wealth.

Here in the mining City of Kitwe
To a locomotive driver at Nkana Mine,
This son of a miner was born
His father hauled and transported the copper ore body
for smelting at Nkana Smelter
Luanshya gave out her wealth
and not to be outdone were Kabwe, Nampundwe
Bwana Mukubwa of Ndola
and Maamba Coal Mines in Southern Province of Zambia.

The giant refineries were among the world's best

Giving fine copper that the world
her power may generate and transport.
Zambia gave and continues to give her copper,
cobalt, zinc, lead, emeralds, gold, coal.
Her cities among the highly urbanized in Africa!

To Wankie (Hwange) they went
Rhodesia (Zimbabwe) took them all
Your coal you gave the world
Boosting your power generation,
production of pharmaceuticals,
ammonia-based fertilizers and other chemicals.
Your trains you powered and yes,
Wankie served you Mother Africa!

South Africa swallowed them too!
Her gold mines (Egoli) wooed the workers
Johannesburg said come
Witwatersrand took them to be the world's
largest producer of gold
South Africa, a place of gold!

And so, Ghana did give her gold too
Kwame, there cried
That your wealth we may all share
And her people to employ
From Kumasi, they came
And from Ashanti they descended
that their destiny they may shape
and their wealth they may enjoy.

And Liberia gave her gold and diamonds

Her people came to mine
From Zwedru they came
And from Tubmaburg they rolled
That Monrovia they may build
And in the share of their wealth they too may bask!

And Nigeria opened up her earth
Her tin, columbite and coal to give
Bitumen, iron ore they explored
Her gold to mine
And from Enugu they came
From Port Harcourt, they emerged
Lagos not to be left out
Her men trekked to work
By their labour, families to support
And none failed to feed their young ones.
For great mineral wealth
your land was endowed with by your Maker
Crude Oil, too, your land gave
To be counted among the world's largest producers
You were to be tagged!

And from Kivu they came
that diamonds, cobalt and copper they would mine
A large and spacious country of Congo DR
The size of Western Europe
Her minerals of Katanga to give
To Lubumbashi and Kisangani, they came
Gold and diamonds to mine
Affluent cities that keep on giving
Trillion dollars' worth of mineral wealth
Congo DR a place they choose to destabilize

that your diamonds they may ship away!
Life of the Congolese you support
From your rich resources
Lualaba River and the Congo River, your blessing
Life from the creator you enjoyed!

Angola, O Angola!
Precious diamonds you give,
Your petroleum never to cease
And so, to Luanda your sons and daughters flocked
To the provinces of Lunda Norte and Lunda Sul
they went
Her mining wealth to explore
Even though your enemy wrestled from your hands
Your diamonds used to finance war – his war
But there, your men went that their life they would
      improve
For my son, you are indeed blessed with wealth!

So too, my other children their mineral wealth they gave
To towns in Tanzania, Gabon, Sierra Leone, Namibia
      and Botswana,
your men flocked
There, your gold, diamonds and other precious stones to
      mine.
The reason I refuse to accept the misconception
That you, my children are poor!
For great wealth under your soil remains still untapped
Africa my continent, Africa the world's richest land!

Aware of my potential of greatness
There came a plan to destroy my future

My land was "owned" by foreigners!
Into another man's hands my wealth rolled
A servant of his I became
My father cooked, cleaned and made tea for him!
He produced for him
From my land, he gave away what was his
For he was told, "His visitor owned all that he saw
    including him!"
A little, my father received as ration
From the window, he bought his groceries
Because the inside of the store was not for him to share.

But Africa is grateful
Grateful that our friends came
That minerals we could mine
and partners we thought we were to be
Ask the Ashanti, they mined gold years
before the Europeans set foot on Ghana
Ask the Lamba, they mined copper too
Years before the settlers came to Zambia
Years before, as my visitors, they came
And overstayed their welcome
And crafts of metal we made
But partners brought technology
Africa is grateful to them
If only slaves they never made us to be!
Slaves and servants for them
Then friends and partners forever we would have been!

Occupied, occupied, occupied!
Africa lives like a nation occupied
Her freedom marginalized

Her liberties swallowed up
by her powerful enemy
The spilled blood of her freedom fighters
still cry for freedom
As a powerful imperialistic force continues
to estrange your children
Demanding more in your labour
Demanding more in your production
Demanding more in your sacrifice
To enrich the powerful international
and multilateral political stooge
who dictates her terms and conditions for your
      prosperity.

Occupied, occupied, occupied!
Once you were an occupied territory,
a colonized territory
Now, an economically occupied territory you are!
Good governance, rule of law, and democracy are
      demanded of you
The one who once ostracized you now chastises you!
He had refused to practice good governance,
rule of law and democracy on you!
Until to the jungle you went
To live with animals, and to share your beds with snakes
Then with a roar you came at him!
Like a lioness robbed of her cubs you descended on him
You refused to rest until freedom was to be granted.

"Equality," you cried
But the enemy saw no democracy!

"Communist! Communist! Communist!" He had roared
    back!
Thousands upon thousands of your fighting
men's lives were exterminated
Your children crushed
Your women ripped open
But a just cause you saw
So, you stood firm and gallantry fought back
To win back your freedom.

But your enemy never gives up
A new machinery of occupation was underway:
Economic occupation!
Your nationalized wealth commanded to surrender
Surrendered for a song
And your workers pruned
Unemployment towers
And suffering unabated
As control of resources he reclaims.

Our situation has been clouded,
Clouded with a lot of burdens,
Burdens of hopelessness and helplessness,
Burdens of hate and vengeance,
Burdens of failure and survival,
Placed on our shoulders by fate and destiny!
But we have refused to bow down to all
We are not the type who shrink and easily
give up nor give in!
We have come a long way baby!
Our fathers sang "We shall overcome some day,"
and they overcame

For no force is too powerful to stop us
Nor, "shall we allow any force to make
us feel like we don't count." [28] (Martin Luther King, Jr.,
    1967).

For our wealth, we shall defend
Our wealth endowed on us by our Maker
we shall protect
But we are willing to share it with the coalition of the
    willing
As long as partners in trade we are made to be or
    recognized!
Mutual beneficiaries to African wealth
For after all Africa knows that no man is an island
Knowledge and technology to exchange
And wealth to share
The creator's wish
That in harmony with one another we all may live.

CHAPTER 12

An Economic Strangulation Exposed!

It is a conspiracy!
A conspiracy of an international capital
Whose wheels of capitalism are moved by the poor
Supporting a machinery that in turn hurts them
Rendering help to a system that kills the weak
It strangulates and suffocates the weak
Through policies that disadvantage the poor
Perpetuated by lending institutions of the rich
To make poor nations of the world dependent
Dependent on the powerful North
That the poor South would continuously
be the source of the much-needed cheap raw materials
that would drive the North's economies.

They force you to print large denominations
of your currency.
Your purchasing power of your currency eroded
5,000, 10,000, 50,000 denominations!
These, they have not in their countries!
When you question back
Through their clenched teeth comes the answer:
"Do it or no aid!"
"Who will print the money?" my children ask

"Paris, France!" "Ottawa, Canada!"
"We have no money in the budget for it,"
my finance minister states.
"A loan! Don't worry, it will be a loan!"
Africa takes another forced loan
that will accumulate enormous amount of interest
enriching the ever profit-driven and weak-capitalizing
Capitalist West!

Unsuspecting myopic leaders of my people concede
At a great cost the money to print
The paper money whose ink peels off
Hardly three months later!
"A plastic (polymer) had been used for bank notes!"
Canadian experts tell Zambia and apologize!
"Treatment not well done!"

Will he discount you for the scandal?
Oh no!
To him you shall go again for a better-quality print
At another great cost!
A tale of business opportunity with the poor by the rich!

Other countries have "soft" currencies
While the oppressors brandish "hard" currencies!
Other countries have "non-convertible" currencies
While the oppressors' ones are convertible!
A mischief and ploy untold
A product of intent
Interestingly, most "soft" currencies are made in
        countries
that possess and brandish "hard" currencies!

But they have not discovered the secret yet
of how to make Africa's currency
"hard enough" like theirs!

I heard Zambia cry
To her children I spoke
That they may tell me what the funeral was all about
Her children told me
"Someone bought off my debts that were to be
    liquidated!"
she sobbed.
$3 million dollars meant to be cancelled by Romania
Bought off by British Virgin Islands-based Donegal
    International
(A US-based Debt Advisory International)
Paid less than $4m (£2m) for Zambia's debt.

And now Donegal sues Zambia for £42m repayment!
"Vulture Fund," they termed it!
$15.4 million that Zambia should now pay the
    "Vulture!"
So, rules the Court!
The UK Royal Court of Justice
(or Court of Injustice depending on your take)
"with additional undetermined legal costs!"
Zambia to pay!
The poor, who failed to pay back the loan of $3 m of
    1979
Must in 2007 pay a company money they had nothing
    to do with!
The vulture to be paid!
And dizzy go my leaders!

For how the game is played, they cannot fathom!

To a London court Zambia is dragged!
The Romanian government too weak to rescue
A game-plan hatched by the rich
The IMF not to protect the weak
For they too know how the game is played
The strong shielded and the weak punished
Another dichotomy of fate for mother Africa!

Why wasn't an arbitrator from Kenya?
Why was he not from South Africa?
Surely, there is a High Court in Abuja!
But to UK, Zambia was sued!
To London, Zambia was dragged
And justice there was expected
From the "UK Royal Court of Justice!"
By the oppressor for the oppressed!

Now Britain abandons the Vulture in 2010!
Wrong, greed and injustice she sees
The real Great Britain, the defender of the weak
    backpedals
Urging the rest of the rich, wrong to see
Her courts not to entertain daylight theft
of the weak and defenceless
Great Britain which pushed for abolition of slave trade
Now the "Vulture Fund" to forego!
For evil, she now sees!
Hail the UK for her bold step to do what is right!

But the step is not wholeheartedly taken

The first country Britain has become
Only registration to limit amounts of debt
that creditors (including so-called "Vulture funds") can
    recover
from heavily indebted poor countries (HIPCs) in UK
    courts
British High Commission to Zambia Tom Carter says,
"This is very good news for countries such as Zambia,"[29]
    (Martin Kaponde, Zambia Daily Mail, June 29,
    2010).
Yes, Mr. Carter, "very bad news indeed!"

It is the usual business story
That capitalizes on the inequalities, deficiencies, and lack
Business and profit motive
Dominance, suppression, and oppression of the poor
Making them once again dependent and not
    independent
A cruel world it is
But the wise and the discerning will
escape the enemy's machinations
Namibia, a success story! No loan no borrowing
From IMF and World Bank
The goose trap for the undiscerning
That traps the unsuspecting
Itself trapped by Namibia!
Those with understanding, will not only expose
but denounce all intents of the enemy as well.

An already squeezed people economically
And a squeezed currency
Made to pay through their nose

At my "Partners in Development" embassies
Exorbitant non-refundable fees in hundreds paid for visa
　　applications!
No guarantee for your visa to be given the day of
　　interview
An exchange rate dictated by outside forces already
　　disfavours you
Your wages not commensurate to what you are asked to
　　pay
Hundreds if not thousands turned away
Their money in thin air disappears!
Never to be seen again!

Should you be eligible to convert your status in his land
Through the nose again you will pay
But you were not allowed to work there!
But thousands of dollars and pounds you are expected to
　　part away with
Maybe to steal from somewhere you are expected!
Should your family be large,
Then I pity you if ever you would make it!
Inequality scales at work everywhere!

For in traps, many other traps lie in wait
To the unsuspecting and often beleaguered poor mother
　　Africa
Her children to feed
Hunger and poverty to avert
So, to "multilateral cooperating partners" she goes
Loans to jumpstart her economy to get
So, she is told
By the "caring international community,"

She is informed
In the event of non-compliance to their policies
In the event of failure to yield to their demands
The act of squeezing your economy to pulp they have
    perfected:
Sanctions, sanctions, sanctions!

Your currency plummets,
Your buying power erodes,
Your exchange rate suffers,
While they laugh in pleasure
A "credit card" policy to apply
Interest rates too exorbitant to be wiped away, –
Calculated at base rates never to match repayment plans!
A deliberate ploy to make me his servant
Mortgaging off not only my land and property
But my children and their children's children!

Zimbabwe, misery, the story untold
Zambia, the plight unannounced
Ghana, the suffering unknown
Congo DR the pain unmentioned
Tanzania, the cry unheralded
Somalia, the sorrow unfathomed
Ethiopia, the difficult unrevealed
Sierra Leone, the affliction undisclosed
And Ivory Coast the shame unexplained
An endless list of my children in agony.

Those with understanding will not only expose
But denounce all intents of the enemy as well.
They shall herald the traps' presence

On the way to passers-by!
Warning the unsuspecting
That the way they may avoid
A path that waylays them
A way mined with traps
To blow off the undiscerning
Injuries incurred too deep, too serious
Not to be remedied in their lifetime
Passed on to posterity
Who knew or had nothing to do with it!

Your tormentors are armed with weapons of mass
        hypocrisy (WMH)!
They majestically walk brandishing them in both hands!
They trick you to sign
"A non-nuclear proliferation treaty!"
If both of us had no nuclear weapons,
It would make sense to sign this treaty!
If both of us had nuclear weapons,
Then sensible it would be!
If one of us has and tells another
who doesn't have or intends to have,
to a treaty to come to sign,
then nonsense it is!

They take your Congo DR uranium
and flood your mines with water
A useless dam they create
That no one else there to mine
Your uranium never to give to another
And Japan mourns!
Her sorrow and pain to be borne for years

As your power mined out of you afflicts the Sunny
    nation
Her children to mourn for centuries
Miseries not to forget.

If I came to your house and took your wife while you
    watched
Because I was the more muscular of the two of us
If I came to your house and I took your wife
Because I was the better armed of the two of us
If I came to your house and I took your children
Because I was deemed the wealthiest of the two
Then you need to be scared of me
When myself I arm
You need to be scared when I cough
You need to be scared when I awake from my long sleep
You need to be scared when I say, "enough!"

If I threw you in prison because you talked back
(For Pharaoh did the same to the Israelites)
If I castrated and incarcerated you
Because a threat I thought you were,
then ask Pharaoh
For a story, he has!
For the Redeemer of the oppressed shall arise for His
    own
For the defenceless He shall speak.

Why has wealth always to be in other people's hands in
    your land?
you ask.

Why must I be made to sell all that is mine to someone
    from afar?
"Privatization," your learned men tell me!
"A key to prosperity," they say.
"Whose prosperity?" my children ask.
"Your country's prosperity," the learned answer.
"A prosperity that never trickles down is no prosperity,"
my young ones observe.
If only my children were able to buy shares like my
    competitors
Then, perhaps we would be talking!
But the rich from afar by virtue of unequal scales,
which work against you always are favoured by the
    system.
The system that yokes you to a life of a perpetual beggar!
Until your technocrats unravel that which holds you to a
    life of dependency
and economical slavery,
an economic slave you will continue to be!

Now to "roll back the zeros" of my currency
My new leaders of the Patriotic Front in Zambia in
    2012 decide
A decision long overdue
A decision long delayed
A bold step of my economists
A decision never to be challenged by the so-called
    "Technocrats"
Who are experts of other peoples' economies
Expertise bent at ensuring a stable economy for
    themselves
And not of others

Expertise bent at ensuring a stable currency for
    themselves
And not of others
Perhaps no opposition, no questions are asked
For there again are printers of my currency
Who lie in waiting
For huge profit margins from the dribble they see
And my children still a step behind they lag!

It is "Rebasing" of the Kwacha so it is called
Money to be printed and minted abroad once again!
Not to be halted for in you profit margins are seen
"Good business prospects" you are termed
A smile to your countrymen once again to return
Days of your Kwacha buying and selling in thousands'
    denominations
to forego
A cry from bankers, Ministry of Finance, and many
    institutions
boggled for years
their budgets and books in trillions they overrun
Yet no corresponding purchasing power the currency
    carries
A rebasing of the currency quickly accepted
By the "International community"
Because the rebased currency will maintain the same
    ratio to the dollar
5,000:1!
For so, says the wise!

And this is no threat, like Kabila's (Laurent).
Who had demanded for a 1:1 ratio with the dollar!

Quickly not to be accepted in Washington and London,
Quickly not to be implemented!
Your guess is as good as mine – He died in a coup d'etat
His plans not to fulfil!
And his "son replaced him!"
And Laurent's plans to the grave go with him!
Tell me, who do you think killed him?

Your National Enterprises
Your governments told not to bail out,
when financial turmoil and bankruptcy threats they face.
The know-it all, masters of economies and self-imposed
      consultants,
your governments they inform
"Bad it is economically that your companies you would
      bail out!"
IMF and the World Bank
stringent measures on you they take
that all your nationalized companies may fail
that to them in the end, you may go
your companies they may buy!

But "what goes around, comes around"
I heard someone say,
"Their motor industries were on a blink of collapse in
      2008,
The housing markets, and their banks, not to mention!"
Unexpected recession knocks at their door
"The Bush-induced recession" not to herald!
Economic stimulus the masters pass!
Their government,
the same who tell you not to intervene in market forces

Their industries to bail out under President Obama!
Indeed, what goes around comes around!
Yet, in their hands you still want your economies to
    entrust
The deceit, up their sleeves you still see not!
O Mother Africa!

CHAPTER 13
BIG POWERFUL WITCHES GO LOOSE TO ANNIHILATE SMALL WEAK WITCHES!

For the big witch goes witch-hunting
That small witches he may find
"Small witches should not practice witchcraft," he orders
For to him alone belong the fetishes
That the world he may hold to ransom
While his fetishes, a stockpile he keeps
Small witches he bullies
That he alone may terrorize and frighten
The inhabitants of the earth.

The big witch enjoys to see
The leaders of the world quake with fear
To their knees they bow
That no evil may overtake them
As they lick his boots
Pleading a cause for peace
Prostrate they fall, to the god of mammon
That it may go well with them
A delightful sight the great witch enjoys viewing
A grin-inducing posture they love to see

'Till they wink at each other with a satisfactory gesture
For the renaissance spirit they have killed
That they alone fetishes they may possess.

One by one, down they go!
Their knees to bow!
Their ingenuity they throw at the masters' feet
Tripoli says, "We surrender!"
"Our fetishes not to harbour or pursue any longer!"
Pyongyang says, "We give up!"
Teheran says, "It is over!"
Pretoria says, "Okay!"
Islamabad and New Delhi not to touch!
Sanctions they cannot call against them!
Isolation, a domain of the few to call
That all may hearken
To the "international community's voice!" so, they say
The same we cannot listen to when "not in our interest!"
When others, other than us make a call!
Interesting this life, my son, it has been!

Leonid Brezhnev had said, "No!"
Mao Tse-tung had said, "I cannot!"
Kim Il-sung had said, "Over my dead body!"
Fidel Castro had said, "Never!"
One by one the East had resisted the temptation to bow
    down
But evil they had courted
The Most High, they had failed to recognize
In their quest for power
And upon the Holy One of Israel they had trampled
Their doom and downfall looming

Danger and defeat lurking at the doorway
For the Owner of Battles was ignored
Now victory an elusive wish has become.

Witches, witches, witches!
Witches hunt for partridges
To slaughter, kill and annihilate,
Fetishes of others to dispose of and destroy
Theirs, to keep and stockpile,
Only them, have unleashed the most potent
and lethal magic on others,
in the history of witches' protracted fight
of outwitting one another to kill.

Their venom unmatched,
their appetite for blood unquenched
On brooms they mount and fly,
Mounting on evil to go and kill,
Flying high to destinations far and beyond,
An outcry they cause and untold pain and misery they
        inflict,
A child from mother,
A father from child, and brother from sister they
        separate,
Anguish and sorrow never to cease.

Clan against clan, a spell to cast
Never again to laugh and share with one another
Your peace, joy and laughter drowned in sorrow and
        anguish
Misery and pain planted for a lifetime
While a party they hold at home,

Annihilation of enthusiastic and ambitious little witches,
They have achieved
A goal and motivation too powerful a delusion
A great witch to dominate,
rule and subject small witches to pay homage to the big
     witch!

One by one small witches their fetishes throw away!
Inspectors from the now irrelevant "World Mother
     Body" to inspect
That small witches are compliant to the big witch's
     demands
The Mother Body herself a witch!
Irrelevant and out of touch with reality
A failed democratic tool for the rich
Under whose budget they run and survive
Charters never independently to observe
Carrying out her master's voice
Of the "Permanent Members" from the witches' block
Who wield power commensurate to the finances they
     put in
That the body's lopsided decisions may continue
The big witches' wishes to uphold
That unlike their competitors,
their powerful nuclear fetishes they may keep.

What security does the "Security Council"
of the so-called auxiliary body of the
"Mother of all Evil" carries?
What terms of reference
that change with the bulldozing of the "elite"
do they follow?

What charter that does not listen to other voices of reason
but to theirs alone?
Witches, witches, yes big witches' Security Council
Or rightly put, "Destabilization Council of the Wicked!"
Erroneously dubbed "UN Security Council!"

"Why tell others that their fetishes be destroyed?"
wonders my late and former Professor of Chemistry
Himself, a veteran!
"Why tell others that 'fetishes' to sting and scald
others with, you are not to build,
while yours you continue to stockpile?"
my amused professor laughs
at the seemingly applied double standards of the big
        witch
His strong fetishes arsenal he continues to build
while others are told not to pursue.
Their ambition not in line with "our interest!"
"Security of the world" to ensure
The truth the world not told
That only to us you all may look
A quick conclusion of war we may always have
Since deadly fetishes only in our arsenals lie!
"You got yours, I got mine too!"
my professor says little witches need to say.

For if witchcraft you practice,
the right to tell others witchcraft not to practice
you have not!
For if witchcraft you practice not,
then, all rights you have to inform others
witchcraft not to practice!

This, a child knows, and so should all adults!

"North Korea, yours to surrender,"
So, says the world's only true voice of reason!
"Iran your wishes to be abandoned
For wrong it is for you to engage in witchcraft!"
So, says the master of witches.
Pakistan not to embrace witchcraft
and your father of witchcraft secrets
to be put under house arrest.
"Libya to hand in little fetishes you must,
that to the broader international community you may
        once again belong,"
so, say us.
And you must listen to us!

Your specialty is to kill the African ingenuity
Killing the African dream is your goal
But none of the African children shall let you escape
        unpunished
None shall scamper and scatter in all directions
At the sight of your seemingly imposing and scary figure
For mighty are the sons and daughters of Africa!
Timid they shall no longer be
With courage and stamina, they will fight back
For winners and champions, they are.

Has the world seen your misery?
Has the world understood?
Can she be an arbitrator for my people
who have been the object of wrath?
Targets of unearned suffering

Targets of calculated destruction and annihilation
Can mortal man be used?
Can he be an agent of extinction of a race,
he had always never wanted?
Did Hitler achieve his goal?
6 million Jews to his credit, he claimed.
Yet like sand on the seashore, they reappeared
Like the flood waters of the mighty Zambezi River
overflowing its banks, they broke out
Scattered all over the globe, they dispersed
And so, shall it be for Africa, my Africa!
Like the waters of the great Congo River, they too, shall
    flourish!

Shall the kings of the earth gather together?
Shall they say in unison, "enough?"
Will they say no to the oppressor?
Do they have enough courage to stop the killer?
Or are they timid and weak?
Afraid of sanctions and pre-emptive military strikes?

But men you are all ye nations!
Why do you stare at one another
while your shame and weaknesses are points
to be used for exploitation by the "champions of
    democracy?"
In your hands are the resources of the world
A great manpower remains at your disposal
And so is the vast land!

But division and ruin you have entertained
A common ground you have failed to strike,

Unity has eluded you
That your common enemy you wouldn't flush out
The new emerging markets are serving as indicators
That everything shall no longer continue
to be limited to the so-called "elite"
For soon the oppressed of the world shall arise
Pity for the once oppressor!

But everybody knows that the conspiracy
will not allow it!
Every self-reliance and development
They would love to curtail
In the name of weapons of mass destruction (WMD).
Yet in their backyard lies heaps and heaps
of weapons of mass hypocrisy (WMH)!
Let all the people of the world arise
For our weapons and currencies
To dance they shall continue
Dancing to the music of the oppressor
But Africa shall no longer accept it
"Enough, enough, enough!" she shall shout.

Once described, "Africa is out of the picture" [30]
    (President George Bush)
Your enemy hoped you would go into oblivion!
Now that a volatile picture has been painted
in both the Middle East and South America
Through a myopic foreign policy
Crafted and implemented by International Capitalism
And motivated not by altruism but by selfishness
A spirit that defends and ensures that only the few
in the world are endowed with riches

And the poor are marginalized and demonized
In them a threat is seen
In them enmity is seen
But now because of a further discovery
of your enormous oil deposits
The microscope is now being refocused
And suddenly "Africa is in the picture once again!"

To learn how to read and write was a crime
punishable by death for an African slave
In the land of the "free" and "liberty!"
A self-taught man to read and write
Booker T. Washington,
a living proof of ingenuity of the power of the mind
Never to resign and give up
That all opportunities in his face lay shut
Because failure he refused to accept
Not to be a last nail into his supposedly
coffin of a failed journey
and a prescribed destiny for him!
And so, an adviser to presidents he became!

To be found courting one of their women was a crime
punishable by lynching
In the land of the "free" and "liberty!"
The "civilized" and "great democrats!"
To be found with my women by authors of such signs as
"No dogs allowed" or "Coloured" was an acceptable
        "normality!"
Yet, Africa continues to make great strides
and great leaps towards her freedom.

South Africa and Namibia, a meandering journey it has
    been
And African Americans a story that makes my side
    cringe!

Her children can read and write
Her ancestors were at the core of this present civilisation
Meticulously denied of their great feat in history
By propagators of hate and injustice
African records of achievement wiped out
Her progress and conquest of the oppressor unheralded
For shame and hypocrisy now stand exposed.

Disinformation and misinformation have been the theme
to destabilize and conquer the weak
Theirs, are camouflaged dictators
Ours, overt ones
Often, created ones by my enemies
that my wealth they may pilfer
Iraq conquest is termed, "Operation Iraq Freedom!"
A desolate place now is!
Libya's overrun is termed, "Libya's Liberation!"
A destabilised land now is!
Syria, chaos not to mention!
Falkland Islands repossessed
A theft of someone else's land!
And in silence the world watches
Protests and demonstrations ignored
Thousands perish and millions wounded and displaced
But does anyone care or listen?

Africa needs no wars

As a continent, you have lost millions of people
by the barrel of the gun
Your enemy's quest for land and riches
left your women ripped open
Your children desolate and your men mutilated
That quest has never ceased
It continues to be the driving force
of your economic manipulation –
a rich market for killing machines
given in exchange with your diamonds.
Kivu, we mourn!

Poverty, disease, and wars continue to besiege thee
Land of my ancestry
"Ebola!" "Ebola!" "Ebola!" They say you have!
Created suffering thrown at you.
"Congo's Ebola outbreak, now concentrated in a gold
        mining area, remains a global emergency: WHO,"
        ABC reports! [31] Morgan Winsor, 2019.
You continue to be the target of unearned suffering
Few realize that you are a product of intent
Tearing you down for your failure to forge ahead
Do they know that your exchange rate
is fixed in Washington and London?
Do they know that they seize for an opportunity
to lend you money?
When natural calamities like drought,
floods, and even unnatural ones like HIV and Covid-19
        (Coronavirus)
Products of intent knock at your door!
The profiteering animal in man is aroused!

For what motive? Africa asks.
"Profiteering from poor masses," they say.
"On what condition?" she inquires.
"That from us you would buy!" they answer.
"And by what means?" Africa perplexingly asks.
"Obviously at an exorbitant interest!"
they, with clenched teeth, reply.
"Antiviral drugs from us to acquire!"
In billions, the cost to run
And my children wonder
if this course was designed in their secret rooms too!

"Wealthy commercial interests from
outside the country–including human traffickers,
kings, colonists, presidents, tycoons, bankers,
mining magnets, arms dealers, mineral smugglers,
elephant poachers, and military leaders–have colluded
with Congolese leaders to loot the country
of its greatest resources … By following the money and
        greed,
we tell the story of how major global events
have driven huge surges in demand for
Congo's riches–from colonial plantation agriculture
to advent of the automobile,
from Industrial Revolution to World Wars I and II
and the Cold War, to the dramatic expansion
of the global weapons trade,
the rise of cell phones and lap tops,
and the mass marketing of electric and hybrid cars,"
John Prendergast and Fidel Bafilemba tell a story!
"Congo Stories: Battling Five Centuries of Exploitation
        and Greed."[32]

What causes wars and strife among the nations of the
    world?
What causes people to rise up one against the other?
What causes bitterness and rage
to be stirred up one against the other?
Is it not hate and exploitation?
When you define who your friend is
When you dictate to him what he can do
and what he cannot do
When you classify him according
to your judgment and experience
By your standards and measuring stick!
When you think you, and only you alone
are more human than others
When you think you, and only you deserve the best,
then wars and strife are stirred!

Pain, sorrow, and trouble should not happen to you
But to your friend, your neighbour they belong
Equality should not be mentioned
Not in goods, in services or as a human!
A false illusion you carry!
When you always look at the negative in your friend
and not the good he bears!
When you force him to think he is inferior
and your children you teach!
When you dehumanize your fellow human being
to promote yourself
When you believe you are the superhuman,
Inferior others are
When you have the ability and capacity to help
but you default.

For fear of equality and being surpassed
always intimidated you!

My mother taught me!
"That there was good and evil in every man!"
"When you constantly look and hunt for evil, my son,
you will surely find it," she had said.
"When you look for good you would get it," she had
    advised.
"My son, learn to look for good in people
and pick up not the bad!" she had taught me.

But my enemy has always seen evil in me!
Even the one who has never been to Africa
thinks we are a tragedy!
Assimilating years of propaganda
Disinformation and misinformation about a good people
A wonderful people
A humble people
A great people
A loving and accommodating people called "The
    Africans!"

Africa is a story
A great story that proves to the world
that it is not what you have
But what they do to you with what you have.
Ghana, the second biggest exporter of gold in Africa
Bears one of the worst exchange rates in Africa!
Send not my children to school
To study your economics
Send them not to school

To study your business
Send them not to school
To study your theorems!

Nevertheless, economic transformers shall come
Sons and daughters of Africa
For out of Africa they shall come
For Africa has learned multiple lessons
Bitter as they may be
That meaningful and sincere development
Can only come from her people
An island though we are not
Collaboration we may seek
But genuine development lies in the local entrepreneur
For in there lies a genuine cause for mother Africa
and plight of her children's children.

What man has the inalienable right and authority
to determine who should rule and who should not?
What man or nation has the audacity and pomposity
of installing a government in another country –
a country and land not their own?
What modern civilisation and law permits and
        authorizes
one nation to dominate and manipulate another nation?
What rule of law, freedom, and democracy
grants one nation to impose its dictatorial ordinances
upon another independent state?

What democracy does not listen to the voice of reason
and concerns of other civilized voices of reason?
For Africa has had her part when the insurgents

and the rebellious have been installed by the rich nations
Planting seeds of rebellion and civil disobedience on
        mother Africa.

Is the hand of the CIA clean in Congo DR?
Who killed Congo's first democratically elected
President Patrice Lumumba following her young
        independence
from the Belgians?
Did his arrogance and failure to "cooperate" cost his life?
The initial blow and support for Dictator Mobutu Sese
        Seko
has never left Africa's giant country any peace!
Like all rich nations of Africa, destabilization once
        planted
has been difficult to uproot!

Is the hand of the CIA clean in Nelson Mandela's
imprisonment and banishment for 27 years?
Who was the catalyst to millions
who had been slaughtered at the hands of apartheid
South Africa?
Your answer should not shock you for
you were once declared by the Supreme Court of a
        country that you
were a property!

Is the hand of the CIA clean in Angola's slaughter?
Africa's once longest war supported by the West
Killing the young independence from the Portuguese
A disputed 1975 victory of Dr. Augustino Neto
A landslide victory turned to a prolonged war

Foolish Dr. Jonas Savimbi lured not
to recognize the incumbent government
To the bush he went and the Bushes followed him!
A 26 years' war between government and rebels ensued
Rebels funded their war clandestinely through diamonds
Which the West accepted and never claimed as terrorists'
     accounts,
all over their territories!
Government used money from oil-sales
A bloody war it was and carnage too huge to fathom!

Millions die, millions maimed!
Proponents of human rights, landmines they supplied
One of the most heavily mined lands in the world,
Angola, my child became!
The landmines, the proponents of peace, refused to ban!
A money-spinning business it is
The same way "life-sapping machines" are not outlawed!
"It is our constitution right to bear arms," they say
And now Angola my child a curse she becomes
Her riches no longer a blessing
The ugliness of battle of ideology takes away precious
     lives
Millions of disabled children, women, and men
Courtesy of the U.S.A.'s refusal to ban landmines from
     the world!
And thanks to the Cubans who came to the aid of
     Angola!

A death toll of 1.25 million people with the maimed
     over 70,000!
Proponents of human rights supplied landmines

One of the most heavily mined areas in the world,
Angola my son became
Over 110 million landmines of different make
And several of them still unexploded!
A curse you became because of your riches
The ugliness of battle claimed 1.25 million lives
Millions of disabled children, women and men
And courtesy of the CIA covert operations
which has claimed a conservative number of 6 million! [33]
(John Stockwell, October 1987).
Shaban town of Kamina, in a stooge of dictator
    Mobutu's nation of Zaire
There, Reagan's weapons to receive
En route to Angola, and a cry in Luanda never to cease!
And in man cruelty you tell me you cannot see!

Who killed Ghana's Kwame Nkrumah?
The ace dreamer of Pan Africanism?
And Thomas Sankara of Burkina Faso?
A dream deferred, a threat postponed but not dead
Implicated in the dreamers' deaths
were the same enemies of Africa!
One strong and united Africa not to have.
Or who was an accessory to the death of General – Dr.
    John Garang?
South Sudan's promising leader wooed and waylaid to
    his death!
Museveni, an installed dictator, protected by powers that
    be!
An accomplice to murder and no finger is seen to point
    at him!
Tutsi hegemony to perpetrate!

Catastrophe, upheavals and disunity, Africa to
     perpetually have!
But the dream was not earmarked to die
Nor was it destined to be quenched
For 45 years later it was to be birthed!
Birthed in the land of the former aggressive oppressor –
     South Africa!
Birthed in full view of those whose hands
are stained with the blood of my children
Sharpeville massacre we remember!
As their supporters watch in disbelief and in
     hopelessness
While they ponder and plan another attack on Mother
     Africa!
Gaddafi the new most vocal one and torch-bearer
Next to pursue!

Slain Mozambiquan freedom fighter
Field Marshall Samora Machel
Revealed a conspiracy in his death
The downing of his plane on the borders
of the then apartheid South Africa
A pure accident or accomplices in his path lay
lurking, his life to obliterate
one whose beleaguered people he had lifted
that one to the grave in sorrow he may go
His down-trodden people in hopelessness to linger.

We love the law and we would love to keep and uphold it
For it is the law that ensures peace and stability
It enforces discipline and respect
for people and their personal property.

It ensures that we live in harmony one with the other.
Therefore, the law is good
But the law that condemns the weak and acquits the
    strong we despise.
The law that protects the rich and tramples upon the
    weak we condemn.
An impartial law it is, and a jungle law
For truth, it carries not
A tool to nail the weak while acquitting the guilty it is!

Proponents of world democratic ideals
With powers to veto!
Proponents of a free and nuclear-free Korean peninsula
With arsenals of weapons of mass hypocrisy in stock
Proponents of a balanced world trade
With an imposed unjust world trade
Proponents of world peace
With sponsored world terrorism
A paradox of world super powers
A confusion to the down-trodden.

The propensity of the rich and strong
World governance to direct
Economies to manipulate
To their advantage
and to the disadvantage of the poor and weak
always it has to be
Equality not to cherish
Ingenuity of others to check
For with power in your hands others to bow down
to you, to the god of money, they should come.
Power never to share

Power never in other hands to give.

Absolute power to retain
That others to you may always look
For power is sweet to have
Power never to let go
Democratic ideals unfathomed
A free and fair society propounded
But a free and fair society we have not!
Wealth and prosperity
Only in a few hands
Wealth and prosperity not to share
That to you alone they may bow down.

World economies, theirs to control
Currencies never to be equal
An economic embargo too cunning to dismantle
Protests at the G8, (G7) G20 not to heed
The cow, they alone may milk
"And ideals of a free, fair, and democratic
society we hold!" so, they claim.
With their hands on their chins,
my sons and daughters perplexedly wonder.
As the stone-faced hypocrisy grins in Africa's face!

Another war, a forgotten war goes on!
Now is Africa's longest war! Over 10 million people dead
And no one cares! Congo War!
Congo DR, we mourn!
A carnage deliberately not to stop
Foreign mercenaries at the heart of it all!
Profit margins to count!

A forgotten war! Congo DR, we mourn!
Uganda, Rwanda, and installed puppet Joseph Kabila in
    Congo DR
Accomplices to the slaughter!
A supposedly Tutsi empire to establish!
A powerful delusion at play!
Concocted in the palaces of murderers, in progress!

Instruments of the carnage in Congo DR
Are masterminded by the rich
Who once had supported a minority group in pre-
    independent Rwanda
To subjugate a people,
A majority group subjected to trauma and humiliation
In a divide and conquer scheme
Now a conspiracy of the trio to steal, pilfer wealth from
    Congo DR
For the powerful rich, is unveiled
And millions to kill in the process
Destabilization and war – a means to milk the cow
One of Africa's richest land left in turmoil
And Africa, deeply sighs!

" 'Deep Cuts' US and European Demand:
Cheap, Industrial, Blood Diamonds –
How Congo Helped Build America and Europe,"
writes John Prendergast and Fidel Bafilemba.[32]
The world's second-largest producer of diamonds in the
    1900s
was and is still a "poor country!"
A poor country by design!
Theft by world's superpowers and suffering by design,

Congo DR still remains today!
Africa, a will power to fight back
she still searches that she would liberate herself
from her oppressors!

CHAPTER 14
AFRICA: MARRIAGE OF CONVENIENCE!

In silence Africa has observed
Sorrow and discontentment, she harbours
Grief and agony, she has borne
Centuries of oppression and injustice to bear
Have her cries fallen on deaf ears?
Does anyone care?
Is anyone willing to intervene or to hear?
Does someone enjoy seeing an organized rebellion?
A rebellion against an oppressive system?
Does mankind ever learn from history?
Bloodshed only to see that we may act.

Like a young woman wooed into marriage
So is Africa before her abusers
Wooed, fondled and molested by her predators
Once used, misused, and abused
Africa is divorced
Sent away with a chain of fatherless children
That she may take care of her little ones
The once lover has left
Gone "AWOL" to a distant land
Little he cares.

Her once upon a time lover forgotten
Their union no love it was
Once allured by his masculinity
That his lust he may pour on the unsuspecting
and helpless woman
His physical satisfaction he may have
Mutual benefits he looked for not
A divorce certificate quickly given, quickly forgotten
For his temporary needs have been met!

Once a Cold War ally
A place for great riches
Once a partner in World Wars
But no more!
A place and recipient of a long-term strife, seed
planted and left forgotten
That Africa and her children the fruit they may eat!
Liberia the forgotten story!
Morocco a station for NATO in wars against Germany
Now a forgotten story!

Tanzania, Namibia, Zambia
There, the Germans to engage!
Congo DR the field of death!
Angola, Armageddon rehearsed!
Kosovo, Bosnia Hesgorvina, Czechoslovakia
Seeds planted, fruits enjoyed!
Iraq, we mourn, a desolate place
Afghanistan weeping to last a lifetime!
Somalia, lawlessness left for a time immemorial!
Angola, now abandoned for now free you are!
Zimbabwe, Ian Smith an ally

Robert Mugabe, a foe!
"And which place haven't you been to?"
my children inquire.

When you say, "Africa is out of the picture." [30](President
   George Bush).
When you say you have no concrete plans for Africa
When you ignore the continent's plight
and plunge it into woes untold,
miseries unheralded
When you take me as an afterthought,
then reserve I the right to question your friendship
Your sudden change of heart
When the chronic amnesia suddenly rolls away
That peace you may share with me.

The alienation of a people
The alienation of a Nation
The alienation of a continent!
Her minerals too precious to exploit
Her coffee too tasty to grab
Her food and fruits good enough but not to order
Her agricultural produce ignored
A trade not to embark on and her people poor to be left
The tropical and subtropical rich and tasty produce
   unmatched!
This too my sons fail to fathom!

When you refused to acknowledge
That my children's sweat was the
foundation of your dream and pride
Their blood the mortar that held it together

Yet into oblivion you wanted to put me
Treated me as though I mattered less
Can I now not question what lies up your sleeves?
That I may know if I can trust you
Your sudden change of heart, perhaps I now can
      comprehend
If in peace you now come
That with me you openly can share your heart's new
      attitudes.

Thank you for the offer to fight the disease
Logic and conscience, an appeal they make
That a good heart they may reach and touch
Resources put together
To fight the scourge that science put together in
      someone's backyard
That an inheritance they may take
That a desolate land they may take
Though thousands go the way of the earth
Millions to dust may go
To the redeemed of the Lord belongs Africa's inheritance
For in integrity they have walked
Their garments unsoiled.

Though not all who have gone
All who are affected by the pandemic
Share in the blame
Some a fault not of their own
But always a remnant He leaves
That His word may always be true
And every man a liar
For some their garments, unsoiled

Their breasts they allowed not to be fondled
Their righteousness they upheld
Not disrobed from their chests was their rampart
Protected by divine grace
For the innocent, He could not let perish
From a deed, not of their own-making.

In holiness they have walked,
In purity they have rejoiced,
And God, their God, has not been ashamed of them
He has promised to cut off their burden and sorrow
Their enemies included.

Now tears of joy shall soon run down the African face
As justice shall run down like a mighty river
That brings healing to a nation
A nation that has mourned for centuries
The warmth she shall feel
It is the warmth that comes from the mother
To her only child under her care
Wrapped in the mother's love
And sorrow and pain shall flee away.

History, experience, and logic
Show that human rights and freedoms
are not granted without a fight!
Even the so-called "Free world"
Had to fight for their independence
Rich conglomerates that own nearly all African
        companies
Survive by giving slave wages to their workers
Only through strikes are meaningful wages given

Montgomery Bus Boycott, a testimony to grants of
    human rights
Unwillingly granted
Fighting, Africa shall never stop
A painful past we share
A common destiny we embrace.

The era of a spineless, ineffective,
and fearsome citizens has come to an end
The new era of bold freedom fighters
and economic liberators has dawned
It was the era that Africa's founding fathers dreamed of
The era that all sons and daughters
of descendants of those who embraced hope and faith
That one day the yoke of slavery
and oppression would be broken
To you we salute
For our civil discourse, cultural, intellectual,
and political life shall never be derailed.

No, they have not heeded to the cry
No, they have not responded to the cry
No, they have not given in to the demand of the
    oppressed
"Now is the time, to make democracy a reality,"[34] (Dr.
    Martin Luther King, Jr.).
Empty words they have been
Falling on deaf ears.
They handpick leaders for mother Africa
And support them through the barrel of the gun
At the cost of Africa's resources
Proponents of democracy!

If prison walls could talk
If the high seas could talk
If the cotton fields could talk
If numerous homes could spill the beans
Of what had happened to the African women –
(Mother and child) while their men
Out in the fields, forced labour they endured
If German atrocities could be recited
In the deserts and plains of South West Africa
    (Namibia).
If the Drakensberg Mts. could talk
If the Orange River could give an account
If the Witwatersrand could lament
At the evils of the Boers on my people in South Africa
And the agonies of slavery.

If Robben Island could sing
Unbearable conditions endured
The excruciating pain untold
Borne by Mandela and company
Oh, if the prison walls could talk!
Of the agonies of the Horse and the Rider!
Kenneth Kaunda and his fellow freedom fighters'
    incarceration
That Northern Rhodesia (Zambia) they would liberate
Oppressed, threatened, beaten but not defeated!
Oh if prison walls could talk!
The deliberate high incarceration rate
of the male child in American prisons!
Oh if only the prison walls could talk!

Oh, if Kenya's "Mau Mau" could herald

Zambia's "Cha Cha Cha" could recite
The agony of many a freedom fighter
Trying to dislodge the British imperialists
If her "BOMAS" [35] could narrate once again (AF
    Acronym Finder. BOMA).
That without "passes"
On your own land, you could not freely travel –
"Colour bar" in effect!
Oh, if the trees could talk!
Of what they saw and witnessed
A true story we could receive
And his story we could not listen to again!

What is the ultimate price for rising up
against a legitimate government?
What is the penalty for conspiracy against an elected
    government
that has been put in place by the people?
What punishment is meted out in any "civilized" and
    "free" society?
Capital punishment or court martial so, they tell me!
What is the penalty for conspiracy
to usurp power from a genuinely elected government?
"Life imprisonment to death," says the international law!

When this penalty is meted out in "developing
    countries"
"A violation of human rights," it is considered
When carried out in "developed countries"
"Justice has been done," they applaud!
Who then has the right
That another government we may judge?

Which then is an impartial judge?
That fugitives and rebels we may judge
Sponsored and trained abroad
That sovereign governments they may usurp!

"I have cherished the ideal of a democratic
and free society in which all persons live together
in harmony with equal opportunities.
It is an ideal, which I hope to live for and to achieve.
But if needs be, it is an ideal for which I am prepared to
    die." [36] (Nelson Mandela, 1962).

With these words, a new home he found
With these words behind bars he went
The words that stunned an apartheid kangaroo court
and its audience
But a cherished ideal they could not imprison
A cherished ideal they could not kill
And Nelson Mandela, an ideal he carried
to Pretoria after 27 years of incarceration.
And a President of a nation he became
One nation undivided by colour, language, and ethnicity –
The Divine's wish.

It is a voice of a "Communist!"
A voice that lacks reason
A voice deserving punishment
If need be, a voice deserving death
A nuisance voice crying out for many
An irritating voice to be silenced
For a voice calling for reason it is not!
A pain in our flesh this voice is!

Erroneously, they were made to believe
But his ascendance to the pinnacle of South African
      power.
His intelligence in discharging of justice
"South African Peace and Reconciliation Committee"
All tell it all, that absurd it is
that for centuries we expounded policies
that were meant to fear one another
and not live side by side –
Dr. Martin Luther King, Jr.'s esteemed dream.

CHAPTER 15
AFRICA:
A PAINFUL TOIL
AND LABOUR THE
JOURNEY HAS BEEN!

Oh, the pain of enduring foreign-orchestrated conflicts!
The pain of enduring foreign-instigated uprisings
The pain of putting up with foreign-supported,
sponsored and backed-rebellions
Rebellions too powerful
An uprising too strong to contain
For on powerful multilateral forces they lean
Removing governments of the people,
for the people, and by the people at will
That an appetite for expansionism they may appease
Unmindful of years of turmoil they plant.

To stop your friend from having what you have is
    immoral
To annihilate him for what he has which you have is
    absurd
To ask him to dismantle what he has
while you stockpile yours is hypocrisy of the highest
    order
To hate a flea and squeeze it to death
because it lives in a land that has plenty
is at the least unthinkable

To dislodge a flea from its territory
in order to have its inheritance is cruelty of the highest
    order
To build a case against a flea to justify its annihilation
though it has no capacity to harm you is injustice
    perpetrated
To love those who don't tell you of your wrongs
and to hate those who point them out to you is to lack
    judgment.

To fail to see logic
and a track record of your injustice to the world
and always blame the other man for your pain is to be
    myopic
To expect the other person always to suffer
and remain poor while you enjoy and get richer
is to lack understanding
To never dreaming of your friend to catch up with you
but to think he shall always be under your bootstraps is
    ignorance.

To hate to love and to love to hate is folly
To help the helpless and to equip the unequipped is a joy
To frown at the poor while you crown the rich is to lack
    wisdom
"A friend in need is a friend indeed."
"Giving to the poor is lending to God."
To share a little with he who does not have is kindness
To tread upon the weak
and to step upon their narrowest hope of survival
is to be brutal.

To ignore the cry of the poor
and to reward them with more agony
is to lack compassion
To love those who love you
and to hate those who hate you
is to be short-sighted.
No man has ever carried his riches to the grave.

To harm the harmless
and to trample upon the trampled is folly
To guide the blind to safety and show them the way
is to store up blessings for yourself
To lead the blind to a trap is to incur a curse
To give to the poor under the guise of kindness
yet expecting to gain more from your gesture
is to be insincere
To have a profit-driven motive and gain
in other people's distress is to be a danger to society
To plant chaos and distress in other people's land
and then watch in amusement afar is to be uncivilized.

Other nations you fought that independence you may gain
Other nations shall fight you that their independence
        they may gain!
Ian Smith of Southern Rhodesia "killed his own people!"
P.W. Botha of South Africa "killed his own people" too!
Dr. Jonas Savimbi killed "his own people" as well.
People he had desperately desired to rule
He killed with the help of foreign mercenaries!
And so, did other pre-independent occupiers of Africa!
But no deliverer we saw!
No friend to bring about our freedom did we see!

That those who "killed their own people"
justice they too would face!

Zambians and other nationals were massacred
in their bid to free the oppressed Africans
A centre and freedom fighters' base she was
Led by the great son of Africa
Dr. Kenneth David Kaunda
That Southern Africa would be free
At the hands of merciless killers, they fell
No intervention by the free world was forthcoming
No condemnation heralded
For coloured were the victims.

Zimbabwe to free,
Namibia to liberate,
Angola from bondage to let go
Mozambique to help rule herself
And in South Africa fascists to defeat
That peace and tranquillity in Southern Africa we would
    enjoy
Kaunda and Nyerere, the sons of Africa
Their brothers and sisters too, to help
Their land with others at peace, they too may live
A vision never to let go until all Africa is liberated.

In a bid to free their people
To the wrong side of the world they found themselves
27 years behind apartheid jail
A lawyer they jailed
A brilliant and intelligent mind they put behind bars
African wisdom and leadership deprived and denied

Others fall by the sword of the oppressor.

But an idea, will, convictions, and dream
Never locked up nor killed
With great intellect and wisdom unmatched
The young freedom fighters mesmerized
their opponents:
"We know through painful experience
that freedom is never voluntarily given by the oppressor,
it must be demanded by the oppressed."
"Justice too long delayed is justice denied."
"If his repressed emotions are not released
in non-violent ways, they will seek expression through
violence,
this is not a threat but a fact of history," –
Prophetic words from the mouth of Dr. Martin Luther
King, Jr., rang.

Lest we misdirect posterity,
Lest we mislead nations of the world,
To them we owe a redefinition of the words,
"Crime against humanity!"
Button-wielding policemen with high pressure fire hoses
directed at a defenceless and unarmed men, women and
children
Crying for equal opportunity in Alabama, Mississippi.
Ian Smith's Rhodesia and Botha's South Africa
Mauled by vicious police dogs
Then the current civilized world has to redefine the words,
"Crime against humanity."
For to them, "all that, they do deserve," so, they say!

An excuse to roll into Iraq to find!
An excuse too strong to justify her occupancy to find
but none could hold any water!
Saddam Hussein to slay, his oil to harvest
For as evil as the inquisition of the Church of Rome was
So, has been the tyranny of "modern man."
"He killed his own people!"
Who has not?
"He built himself good mansions!"
Who has not?
"He attacked another country and took it!"
Who has not?
"There are so many poor people in a rich country of his!"
Which rich land has had no poor people?

The record that Europe and America has had on Africa
     is overt
The blood that drips from their hands is still fresh in our
     eyes
The pain they have inflicted unbearable
The wounds we carry "unbandageable!"
The sorrow they had brought unforgettable
The misery they had left unpalatable.

The great wealth of our enemies
is used to sway Africa and other countries' economies
Bringing my mother to her knees
with orchestrated depressions
For their institutions control the world's wealth.
"Their Security Wings" sponsoring or initiating virtual
     chat sites and websites
to sway countries' political landscape and opinion

To incite violence or plant disorder
To unseat governments!
Unsuspecting populace falling into traps unseen!
Their countries on fire they set!
To the amusement of the enemy!
While in ignorance, our people one another they butcher!

A preacher once roared,
"If you look like me in this auditorium,
then at risk you were born."[37] (A preacher in Columbia,
    South Carolina).
Like Moses in Egypt, born at risk
A threat he was, and so were other males
In some countries prison doors remain ajar
And so, does death
That in them you may crawl
All males born at twice the risk
Confinement a means to control the "coloured" race
A means to control the unwanted species' population.

For now, procreation will bring forth
a vulnerable group of children
With no role model to look to
At risk, they become
Making someone wonder if the "New Disease"
falls in the same category
The category of population control!

Like their predecessors another generation is brought
    forth
Whose fathers live locked up behind bars
With no fathers to guide

Rebellious children they become
Everyone looks down upon them
Fathers, they do not have
products of single parentage
Emotionally broken and scarred are their lives
A fault partly of our own.

Nevertheless, history and cruel intents
cannot be ruled out completely
A perpetual wish to fragment the African family
But fate and destiny lay not in their captors and
        tormentors
But in the Holy One of Israel
and better choices in our hands
That the cycle we may terminate
A cycle of doom and despondency.

Why do you fall into the trap, O Africa?
Why do you love to sell your beautiful bodies around?
Why don't you hold your jobs together?
That education you may pursue
That pleasure and entertainment you may despise
And so, a waylaid trap you may tread not in
And that you may spare yourselves from miseries untold.

The person who tries to take away your pride
is your enemy;
The person who robs you of your sense of pride
and dignity is a murderer,
Causing you to lose your morale
Demoralizing and traumatizing you
That inferior you may be made to think you are

And that you do not count
Though Africa prides herself with her greatness
Tall she stands in the midst of evil forces
that are mobilized against her.

Africa should not and cannot be forced to democratize
When the institutions of the rich remain autocratic
Africa cannot be forced to democratize
So as to make it easy for the rich to manipulate her
For funding of the opposition and surrogate
        governments
is not democracy!
Usurping of power from the majority is not democracy!
First, remove the log in your eye, then the splint in the
        African eye!

We cannot be bought,
We cannot be forced,
We cannot be persuaded,
And we cannot be coerced,
To always do things the way they are done where you live!
Yes, Africa can learn from you!
But her affairs Africa can direct
If only you would let her do so!

My mother taught me
While still young and a delight of women to hold
"My son, listen to me," she had said.
"A businessman takes full advantage
of the inequalities and loops in the economy
the so-called demand and supply
to exploit and further his business!"

Then I discovered what my mother
had taught me years before
I heard him (my tormentor) say,
"Market forces should dictate the price!"
As a clever businessman, he knows whose head will hang!

My son, a prophet of our time
In non-violence, he believed
That the earthlings would heed
A preacher of love and reconciliation
That in harmony we all may live
A teacher of masses he was
He tells the world:
"It is right to tell a man to lift himself by his bootstraps,
but it is cruel just to say to a bootless man that he ought
        to lift himself
by his own bootstraps. It is even worse to tell a man
to lift himself by his bootstraps when somebody is
        standing on his boot."
Washington DC March 31, 1968 [38] (Dr. Martin
        Luther King, Jr. Stone of Hope, Columbia, South
        Carolina. Words, 1968).

"I just want to do God's will, and he has allowed me to
        go up
to the mountain and I have looked over
and I have seen the promised land.
I may not get there with you. But I want you to know
        tonight,
that as a people we will get to the promised land," –
April 3, 1968, assassinated April 4, 1968 [39] (Dr. Martin
        Luther King, Jr.).

"The oceans of history are made turbulent
by the ever-rising tides of hate. History is clustered
with the wreckage of nations and individuals
that pursued that self-defeating path of hate.
Love is the key to the solution of the problems of the
         world.
Injustice anywhere is a threat of justice everywhere."
April 16, 1963[40] (Dr. Martin Luther King, Jr.).

A mammoth task lies in your path
A task to reverse centuries of asset-stripping
and pilferage of your wealth
A concoction of a self-proclaimed elite
and masters of the universe
Through machinations of evil, international bribery
and murder.

The wheels of change for Africa's independence were
         unstoppable
The wheels of change for the former Soviet Union
were unstoppable
The wheels of change for desegregation and civil rights
were unstoppable
And so, shall the wheels of change for Africa's
economic empowerment:
For whoever shall stand in her way
Shall the wheels roll over him
For history, indeed, repeats itself
Fools never learn from it
But the wise apply themselves to it and learn.

He forces you to implement conditions

in trade that disfavour you and favour him
He forces you to privatize all your companies
and to remove exchange controls on all your goods!
He orders you to go "Free Marketing!"
He says a free market economy
is the answer to your ailing economy
It will certainly remove you from your doldrums.
Doldrums that have engulfed you
"Liberalize your economy!"
Meaning sell us your assets!

But in his country
Exchange controls remain to hold his economy together!
A heavy penalty is given to violators of his exchange
        control
Stringent measures that protect his economy
are ever in place
Making sure that Japan's interests are checked!
China's shares remain constant
Canada's business is favourable
That his economy is hurt not!
Farmers' subsidized!

A different scenario for Africa!
And Africa, like a prostitute,
prostitutes herself to her master
Who rapes and defiles her economy
That more and more cheap goods
they may haul
An unfair and an imbalanced trade
they may advance
Exploiting my mother's wealth

By a crafty and selfish powerful force.

Who said the Scramble for Africa ended in 1900?
Africa's partition ceased centuries ago?
For a continent under siege
she continues to be
Her wealth distributed among the greedy few
who continue to terrorize the minds of the innocent
The populace under siege
Unknown to them is how they could have the siege
      broken!

CHAPTER 16
DEMOCRACY GOES TO THE DOGS!

Now democracy has gone to the dogs
The right to your personal opinion it used to teach
(so, I was taught)
Respect to your personal opinion it used to uphold
(so, I was informed)
The role of your personal expression it used to propound
(so, I was lied to!)
But the barrel of the gun is now advancing it!
Exported unconventionally
With pre-emptive strikes on sovereign nations
it is being advanced.

"Democracy was a rule of law,"
So, I was told
"A difference of opinion it allowed,"
So, I was taught
"A tolerance for opinion of others it espoused,"
So, I was informed
"Other people's opinion it also respected,"
So, they had said.
Alas!

My view is not always right!

His view is!
And always it will be
According to his opinion
Another paradox of fate.

Oh, how unpalatable it now is!
To watch your once glamorous leader
Disrobed before multitudes!
Humiliated before millions
and paraded on the box
To the laughter and joy of the imperialist's voice
and media!

"Millions he killed!" they say
But millions they have killed too
And they have forgotten!
"He annihilated his own people!" they shout
But assassins they had supported
Insurgents they were,
and insurgents they support all over the world!

Uprisings with roots from them we have seen
Rebellions sponsored, insurgents planted
Discovered and paid by the enemy
Collaborating with the enemy
who plants lifelong ills and chaos!
Like pawns on the chessboard
so are these dissidents
Unknown to them that their countries
to the god of mammon, they have sold
Advanced to cause anarchy and confusion
That the master the oil and minerals he would inherit!

Nations of the world stay akimbo
Their tails they tack
at the roar of the great
Their heads in sand buried
As though nothing they have seen
They quake at the appearance of the unjust
and self-proclaimed liberators
Filthily rich and armed to the teeth they are
Their reign of terror echoes all over the world
At the sound of their supersonic crafts.
With craftiness, the world opinion is swayed
all nations of the world are terrified
The noise of their WMD send all to hide
As shivers run down their spines
The unjust king no one to condemn again!
Saddam once a glamorous leader his life snapped away!
Gaddafi's imposing life follows him!

We don't tell them what to do
But they always tell us what to do!
We don't tell them what should be done
But they always tell us what should be done!
We don't tell them what has gone wrong in their
        countries
But they always tell us what has gone wrong in ours!
We don't tell them how to fix their economies
But they always tell us how to fix ours!

Solutions they have for South Africa
Solutions they have for Zambia
And solutions they have for Zimbabwe, Ghana, and
        Kenya

Solutions to problems they had initiated
Yet palliative has been the treatment
For no curative treatment shall they give
For there, lies their gold
That with their empty bowl they may tap.

An independent state Zimbabwe is
There, Tony Blair holds no jurisdiction
An independent state Great Britain is
There, Robert Mugabe holds no jurisdiction
No mandate has any
that each may instruct
how the other state should be run!
Africa has not told you how to run your countries
Nor would you ever respect that order!
So, the voice of Africa says
"To hell with your insinuations!"

Where now is the god of democracy?
No true democracy can ever exist
amidst unbalanced scales!
Pressurized to repeat the vote by external forces
is Turkey!
Her parliament votes against use of her airspace
to launch strikes against a neighbouring country!
To her they say vote again!
America's presidential election's result
contrary to public opinion
cannot be forced to be recounted!
A long tale of Western hypocrisy!

With craftiness

the world's opinion is swayed
With craft intent, they lie to the world
and the world questions them not
For in them and with them are the "know it all!"

A relay race you are made to run
An outer lane they give you
An inside lane they get
A quarter of a mile ahead of you they start
Your lane they expect you to keep
A heavier button than theirs you carry!
A yoke they fasten around your neck
On your shoulders, burdens you carry
And so, does your back
Hundreds, yes thousands of hurdles they place in your
    track
Competing in the race with them!

In amazement and awe the crowd watches
and cheer or jeer?
As hurdle after hurdle you are made to surmount
Sweat and perspiration drench your body
In disbelief and concern they watch
At the crafty and unfair fellow competitor, you have
His lane, shorter and smooth
Yours long and crooked
with weighted burdens,
Competing in an unfair race.

The intermediary and judge
To their side he is
Rules for the race together they created

No lawyer you have
No court to turn to
For the International Court, a stooge she is
With smiles and ease
They compete with you
A mother of burdens you are
Victory for themselves they see
For great are your burdens
And numerous are your hurdles to cross.

Hostile is the field you run on
Hostile is the crowd which watches
Hostile is your fellow competitor
And hostile is your judge
Hostility is the name of the game
End of hostility, end of favourable business for him!
So, hostility he shall keep creating
That well it may go for him!

More hurdles Africa to meet on the way
More hurdles erected on your way to cross
That your way it may not go well
The crowd mesmerized
As they watch you cross hurdle after hurdle
But no help to render.

"Shall anyone remove the hurdles?"
the crowd asks.
"Shall anyone break the yoke for you?"
they inquire.
"Shall anyone remove the burdens
off your back and shoulders?" they sigh.

"Would anyone bring the competitors
to the same starting point and equal lengths of lanes?"
they ponder.
But who is the just arbitrator?
That to him we may turn.
The just and impartial lawyer,
that to him we may present our case.
Yes, and Africa deeply sighs!
Competing in an unfair race!

CHAPTER 17

A Shame Sometimes We Have Been!

Sometimes foolish we have been
Sometimes a disappointing lot we have been
Our conduct something not worth to write home about
To the fruit of lawlessness, we have eaten
And pathetic our life has been
Our values to the dogs we have decided to throw
Pouring contempt on our highly esteemed culture
By embracing that which is shameful and repugnant
In the misguided belief of civilisation and development.

A disgrace to the world and to our Maker
we have been
When to walk naked we have chosen
When to lurk at every corner we have loved
When we have decided to exchange
sexual partners like dogs
Fathering children at will
Babies we cannot look after
Our babies we turn to our mothers,
our grandmothers that they may look after
Foolish we have been.

Sometimes foolish we have been

Sometimes a disappointing lot we have been
Our lifestyle something not to emulate
To the fruit of deception, we have eaten
And pathetic our lives have been
A disgrace to the world and ourselves we have been
When our bottoms we choose to sag and expose
When at every corner we lurk
Taking in every intoxicating beverage
Smoking every illicit drug
And pushing in every mood-altering material
A disgrace we have been.

Sometimes foolish we have been
Sometimes ignorant we have been
Sniffing, smoking, and pushing in drugs
From a sponsored cartel, drugs to buy!
Unknown to us, a trap waylaid not to see!
Imported cocaine into your community
By powers that be, not seen!
A destruction of a community unheralded!
Sentences for crack cocaine and powder cocaine,
        dissimilar!
A fair sentence not to see!
Crack cocaine your people jailed indiscriminately
Powder cocaine, his people a near free pass given
A cartel of a supplier jailed once he has outlived his
        usefulness
A destruction of a community achieved!
His money not to see any more
And your poor myopic children, a set up not to see!
For indeed, sometimes foolish we have been!

Sometimes foolish we have been
Sometimes a let-down we have been
Our conduct has betrayed those who brought us forth
A disgrace to our mother
And a shame to our father
When cursing becomes our daily language
And when despising anything that is good
becomes our nature
A disgrace we have been.
When hip-hop and sex seem to be all we live for
and desire, –
Rap, our food to chew
And reggae our drink to swallow,
A disgrace we have been.

Sometimes foolish we have been,
Sometimes a humiliating lot we have been,
When reasoning we throw to the dogs
A disgrace we have been.
Like animals we live
A disgrace we have been
When family values we no longer cherish,
A disgrace we have been.
When rebellion we choose
A disgrace we have been,
When identity, value, pride,
and self-respect we lose,
A disgrace we have been.

Sometimes foolish we have been,
Sometimes a shameful lot we have been,
Our conduct unpalatable it has been

When our youth we lose
A disgrace we have been.
When our teachers we curse and disrespect
A disgrace we have been,
When our music becomes detestable to listen to
And foul in content it is
A disgrace we have been.

An exclusive problem of the West
Destroying a people.
Imported into Africa – courtesy of the despicable movie
    industry
Their roots to remember no more
Their history forgotten
A meaningful, progressive conversation
they cannot hold
Divorce, a looming enemy that awaits
the newly-married
Their children vulnerable to destruction
Sent on their way to ruin
And the youth given to vanity
Yes, sometimes a disgrace we have been!

Righteous living they shun
Uprightness they dare not mention
Moral living their leaders never mention
Man and woman, a holy matrimony – politicians
never expound
There, they fear to tread where none should tread
To win all to themselves
At the expense of the living
No guide to lead

No mentor to follow
And catastrophe lies in waiting
As everyone lives as he sees fit
A destruction to the world envisioned.

When beyond sex we fail to live,
An embarrassment we have been;
When beyond the bottle we fail to live
A let down we have been.
When beyond drugs we fail to live
Fools we have been
When jobs we fail to keep
A shame we have been
When correction we have failed to accept
and our parents we have disrespected
Good for nothing we have been
A gross misrepresentation of Africa we portray
And gross injustice have we done to ourselves!

When our youthful energy we spend
on something unprofitable
Short-sighted we have been
When our precious time we have wasted
on something that does not build or edify
Fools we have been
When our future we choose to shred
Headstrong we have been
When to hang around with folk going nowhere
we choose
Failure we choose and fools we have been.

When to hold yourself together you fail

A slave you become to your enemy
When to hold yourself together you fail
A profit margin you become to your tormentor
When to hold yourself together you fail
A competitor you cease to be
And enter you into his annals of history, his story,
As "statistics of a failed generation."

With metal your body you pierce
A disfigured look you promote
Colours and shapes on your beautiful, gorgeous
and handsome bodies
"Tattoo" you call it!
A repugnant deed to the eyes of your Maker
An abomination to your Creator
Your beauty destroyed.

A covenant with the evil one you enter into
And you know it not!
Turning your back on your Creator
Your only hope to redeem you
From an endless oppression, you face
That of physical and spiritual despondency.

Your walking away from Him never satisfies
Your rebellion against Him never an answer
Reasoning with Him, your only hope
Wisdom and peace, the only One to grant
That your family may be orderly
For hopeless you are without Him
With Him, all to conquer
For great is your enemy

And many are those against you!
Yes, sometimes foolish we have been!

Liberia, a "Land of liberty and freedom!"
Freedom to elude
Established by free slaves
From the land of the free
"Land of liberty and freedom" to create
A failed dream
The freed slaves and their descendants
The natives of the land not to mix
An assimilation not to embrace
For evil is in the heart of man
No colour it knows
The Creator's pronouncement.

Oppression knows no boundaries
It can be perpetuated by black or white
By yellow or brown
From an uncircumcised heart comes evil
Educated men on the uneducated
to discriminate
The rich against the poor to trample upon
One ethnic group against another to annihilate
One nation against another to ruin
A selfish heart and attitude of fallen man
Only from his creator selfishness to blot out
Education, man's education
foolishness of heart not to cleanse.

Rwanda, a case study of evil of man
Burundi not to forget!

Evil which knows no colour
Tutsi against Hutu and Hutu against Tutsi
Brother against brother
Supremacy – not moved by colour of one's skin
Superiority complex motivated by ethnicity
A disgrace to mother Africa.
Thanks to a now matured seed left by the Belgians to
    sprout!
In the divide and rule or conquer hegemony!

In Congo DR, Rwandese never to assimilate
Rwandese in Congo DR
not with locals to embrace whole-heartedly
A planted group to be used to destabilize another nation!
A people never to mix with others
But Africans we all are
A problem of the heart of man
Not caused by another race different from us
A people prone to man's sinful nature
Somalia, "Somali Bantu" not to accept by "Somalis"
Segregation deeply rooted from colonial era and slavery
Arabs to propagate marginalization
Britain and Italy to prey on
Sudan to continue to suffer from the scourge
Nigeria, an inheritance too deep and too complex to
    thwart
Religion and land to complicate it even further
And divided Africa remains to date!

The one with a lighter skin
feels he is superior to the other with a darker skin!
The one with a darker skin subjected to hate himself!

Features like those of a flower from the creator to hate!
Ignorance and foolishness deeply inculcated
Fed and nourished through years of enslavement,
marginalization, and stereotype.
Our sons and daughters learn from the delusional forces
of marginalization and discrimination!
For indeed, foolish sometimes we have been,
That a lie we have chosen to believe
And failed to see that one people we are!
And one people we will be!
Indeed, sometimes foolish we have been!

To those who divide us we pander
With them we work, undermining our countries
Leaders, kickbacks they obtain from our enemy
South Africa, Southern Rhodesia our own blacks with
        the enemy they fight
Against their fellow blacks to kill
A name they seek to coin for themselves
Bought with money, money they will never take to the
        grave
Killing their own keen to the shame of Africa
For indeed, sometimes foolish we have been.

CHAPTER 18
THROUGH DECEIT TO BE ENSLAVED AGAIN!

South Africa they lure
That "homes" for the poor they may build
Through debt to build
"A concern for the poor they have!" so, they say!
A disguised scheme they propose
That a perpetual debt South Africa may incur
A nation under bondage soon to be
Her children an endless debt they may inherit
To a bothersome international capital, they may owe
In their lifetime, never to be repaid.

A rule of trickery they employ
Influential, ignorant African men with
Western education they use
That at the table of negotiation they may sit
Their African governments they may persuade to sign
Lobbying on behalf of their master
That their signatures they may append
Their countries the leaders may mortgage
To the international capital
With kickbacks, they meticulously
may sell-off their offspring.

To their governments they lobby
"The necessity" of the loans to get
In doom, the leaders once again append their signatures
My children yoked again forever to usurer.

Eligibility for further debt relief
is greeted with further conditions
A predicament unbearable for Zambia
A grip too tight to untangle
After entry of the enhanced
Heavily Indebted Poor Countries (HIPC) initiative
in November 2000
The promised "manna" from IMF and World Bank
of reaching the "completion point"
A point of debt relief delivery in 2003
A huge external debt of $6.8 billion
relieved up to half the amount is promised!

Alas!
The rules of the game were once again changed!
In spite of the good track record of repayment
Confirmed by IMF and World Bank
The Multilateral master dribblers
"discovered" Zambia was not meeting the benchmarks!
Limitations on public sector salaries set by the Fund
were not being met!

To a Staff Monitored Programme (SMP) instead,
Zambia is put until June 2004!
Consequentially, from the
Poverty Reduction and Growth Facility (PRGF)'s grace
    Zambia fell!

The "completion point" eluded!

Therefore, Zambia would be required to pay US$300
  million in debt

An amount to be serviced from domestic resources in
  2004

The figure skyrocketing in latter years!

For decades half of her GDP has been servicing these
  loans

Every year never to default[41] (President Kenneth Kaunda
  personal communication, 2003)

Half is used for non-existent capital projects,

Road maintenance and construction and medicines in
  hospitals

Yet they have the audacity to ask why we are poor!

Every African country has a similar story!

Nigeria mortgaged!

But Dr. Ngozi Iwuoha, Finance Minister dribbles the
  learned!

My child with her highly educated personnel

Never to let down her nation!

A buy-back proposal wipes out Nigeria's Paris club debt

and reduces the country's external indebtedness from
  $35 billion to $5 billion

So, to pay back the debt with cash she decides!

IMF and World Bank, Nigeria not to be bothered again!

The power of usury

and international credit card to the unsuspecting poor

disgraced and broken!

Masters at the cheating game beaten at it

And Nigeria finally frees herself from

International conmen

who ply their trade in New York and Washington!
For my son Nigeria is blessed with the educated!

Namibia a showcase of Africa's ingenuity
Sam Nujoma not to deceive
A freedom fighter on the field of war and a freedom
      fighter in economics
Deceit and bribery never to court
Free from enslaving "credit cards"
Which the IMF and World Bank call "loans!"
Unaware to African leaders that mortgaging their
      countries
lay at the heart of their "goodwill partners!"
Who through deceit were masters of control
And your countries to own again
Subtly appending their signatures to economic bondage!

CHAPTER 19

ECONOMIC LIBERATORS WE NEED!

Africa is in dire need of economic liberators
The likes of Robert Mugabe
That their countries they may not sell
Their countries dear they may hold
Their continent dear they may hold
And Africa they will dictate
Out of her current quandary
Fixed and designed by the self-proclaimed
"democrats and liberators"
But at what cost would these,
our "dictators" come?

Museveni, the real dictator has a free pass
So was Mobutu
Since to his tune, both men danced
Their "human rights" record nothing to write home about
But a pass they get
Dancing to the tune of their masters
That to power they may hold
Different scales used!
And Africa never ceases to be amazed!

To wars they go

That resources they may control
And to bondage they may keep
The conquered and the vanquished to subject
Misery and suffering to usher in
Never to leave in your lifetime
Strife and pain forever planted
While they prey on your resources!

Your wealth to pilfer
Your goods and services under their control
Poverty and lawlessness, they plant
Divide and rule
An old tale you are familiar with to uphold
A game for centuries played
Africa's adversaries employ.

Rwanda, a genocide remembered
African against African
They senselessly butcher one another.
While their masters watch
Capable hands to stop the carnage kept at bay
At the order of their foreign governments
Akimbo, the UN sits
Watching the dying under their noses
As years of divide, conquer, and rule come to play
A seed planted by the Belgians now to mature
Their men they evacuate
A slaughter of children, men and women left behind.

9% Tutsi population deliberately put in power
The Belgians' intent to subjugate
The majority Hutu subjected to abuse

A policy of divide and conquer to play
Military, government posts, the Tutsi to hold
Decades of segregation birthed and propagated
by a foreign power
The majority in silence suffer under unbearable
   autocratic rule
Abuses of a people by another
Soon independence to overturn the tables,
the colonial power envisions
For under a majority, the Hutu would obviously come
   to rule!

Now in a hurry to make amends
with the vanquished to meet!
That peace they may broker for!
The Hutu to convince,
that retributions never to exercise after independence
on their kin!
A report on the issue, the Belgians, in fear of their deeds
   to the UN
they write before their unceremonial departure
A catastrophe they had sown for years soon to mature
And none holds the perpetrators of hate accountable!
When aflame the country, consequentially, burns!

The interest, their interest
Is not in you but your wealth
The interest, their interest
Is in your goods and minerals
They plant seeds of animosity among you
The catalyst to their enrichment
While busy you keep annihilating yourselves like fools

"Tutsi" or "Hutu" you call yourselves
A people divided by hate and hatred
A shame to Mother Africa you are!
Paul Kagame to power to hold firmly
Tutsi dominance over a majority to propagate again
And a dictator not to be called
For him too, to his tune he dances
And peace Rwanda once again to elude!

To the sword his subjects he keeps
Allowing no room to think for themselves
"Brainwashing," the theme to be
That for everything to him they may look
This, a product of personal dependency
A syndrome concocted and approved by your mentors'
    institutions
Created with a false illusion of hope
For no such institution could ever take you
out of your current doldrums
Which your enemy has created for you!

Sudan, a tale of shame to share
Brother against brother to rise against
Ideology and religion to separate them
Colour of skin to distinguish them
An inheritance never to share
A now mature seed planted by colonialists
A product of divide and rule
Never to obliterate
Hate of brother by brother
And a shame not to tell.

Sudan, my largest nation
A tale of sad news
News to break my back
Tears never to stop flowing
Sudan my child
Why had it to be you?
A confluence of history, politics, land, ideology,
religion, and wealth at loggerheads!
Ethnicity and language not to tell
Her children abroad to scatter
Running away from a marauding lion of the north
With unclean teeth
Her own blood to devour
Her appetite for blood not to quench
Sudan, my child!
Why had it to be you?

To a religion of hate you succumbed
One whose theme of love never to know
Love, the golden rule espoused by the Christian South
never to embrace
Janjaweed, a marauding lion in human form to hate
Coming from the north their fellow brothers to hurt
Darfur mourns!
Women to rape, children and men alike to put to the
        sword
And Islam, the so-called "religion of love," evil never to
        stop!
50 years of common sense and reason
not to heed
Now a divided state you are
South and North Sudan you become

Charles Kapungwe

Sudan my child
Why had it to be you?

Oil, your curse, must have been
"Black gold" a curse for the nations, indeed is!
Inviting your enemy
From afar he comes
His interest to invest
Riches to tap
Divisions to plant that oil may easily flow out
While busy at one another's throat you go
And the cleverly instituted machinery
you see not!

Riek Machar, apparently, like Dr. Jonas Savimbi,
his education to the dogs to throw!
Courted by opportunists, South Sudan to sell!
Greed and power at the centre of it all
The weakest link, my enemy, in you opportunity
to control and oil to see!
Unmindful of the carnage of human life to annihilate
China, to be prevented at all cost
South Sudan oil exploration not to pursue
And even the educated blinded!
For a shame now it is!
Now, it is not the Janjaweed but one of you leading the
      slaughter
Like a pawn used and you care not!
Exploitation of ethnicity and power, our enemy to
      utilize
O South Sudan, my son, I mourn!

Nigeria, O Nigeria!
The same tale and fate you have!
Religion, land, and ethnicity exploited
By the Horse and the Rider
Years of British rule divide and conquer waged
The poor Islamic north empowered shrewdly to rule
The rich South subjected to underdevelopment
and control
Wealth from the South to tap
but the north to develop!
Now Boko Haram a nuisance among you arises
Annihilating life at will and shame is not felt!
Nigeria my child, I mourn!

Brandishing arms, your people to terrorize!
Arms not made in Abuja!
A paper trail for money laundering they can locate
But the source of arms is "too complicated"
for lovers of democracy to find!

Years of inequalities,
Unfortunately, even current governments
never to correct!
Seeds of animosity planted for decades
not easy to be undone!
Leaving the Islamic fundamentalists
an opportunity to thrive on.
Who shall stop the carnage?
Only a new breed of leaders
bent on undoing an economic bondage
A product of design
can take you out of this political and economic quagmire!

Somalia! O Somalia!
"A failed state," you are called
A product of history and fate
A nation divided by political powers and ethnicity
Seeds of fragmentation too deep, too complex to undo!
Exacerbated by religion and fundamentalism
A divide too complex to unravel!
Political will lacking and intolerance and hate your
        downfall
Blessed with a great frontier of a coastline
But never put to good use, your enemies' quest!

A strategically located gateway to the Middle East and
        Far East
To Europe and North Africa not to mention!
To pirates you look and your hands to produce wealth
        you discard
Political unrest and murder become your theme
A shame to your mother Africa you have been!
For to reconcile your differences you lamentably failed
And new economic liberators
and sound spiritual leaders
pointing you to the Saviour of the world you lack!
But to Al-Shabaab terrorists you succumb!
To Islam you turn but peace to elude you
For only the Son of Man grants true peace.

Who will take away this disillusionment
and disappointment from our people?
Who will wipe away this doubt
and desperation from our children?
Who will roll away this disenchantment

and dissatisfaction in my soul?
Who will erase this despondency
and destitution of soul?
Somalia left busy to destroy one another!
A country in turmoil it is!
Left in confusion so it could not develop and produce oil
Your "brothers" in the Middle East
supporting the terrorists so that only them can be
        exporters of oil
And you foolishly remain blind!
Your country to tear apart!

Africa, a tragedy meticulously designed,
A tragedy meticulously executed!
Show me a tragedy that his hand is absent
and gold I will give to you!
Africa, a catastrophe craftily penned
A catastrophe craftily carried out!
A land of procurement of goods and services
A land of finished goods to import!
A land that feeds all
Her raw materials raped for a song!
Goods paid for,
with money that cannot pull you out of your quagmire
nor your perpetual loans not to be serviced
For the "International Community" you owe
And at their disposal you lie.

Show me a catastrophe of a nation
that his scheme is absent
And with rubies I will reward you!
Show me a war on the continent you see

that his hand is not in
and with emeralds I will reward you!
Ivory Coast, a once glittering gold of West Africa!
A leader in Laurent Gbagbo who to the enemy's tune
     refuses to dance
An end of his chapter comes
His reign, cut short
And therein come French troops!
Leaving me wondering
if ever my troops could step in his land uninvited
and with no visa to show!
Economic bondage to perpetuate!

Show me a calamity of a nation
that his devise is absent
And silver I will grant you
Grenada, Uganda, Zimbabwe, Congo DR, Mali,
Sierra Leone, Angola, Libya, Egypt, Somalia, Eritrea,
Rwanda, Burundi, Congo Brazzaville, Cuba,
Venezuela, Argentina, Panama, Iraq, Colombia, Mexico,
     Afghanistan,
an endless list.
The anguish and pain of affliction by design
Affliction and pain by intent
While the world, akimbo, it watches
In disbelief and fear at the bully and the mighty
Who strangle and annihilate the weak
and the defenceless of the world
while those with power to undo
the perpetrators of injustice,
watch without much ado
Unwilling to come to the rescue of the weak!

African economy to rape!

An economic liberator you need
Kwame Nkrumah gave Ghana her independence
Julius Nyerere gave Tanzania her freedom
And Kenneth Kaunda gave Zambia her liberty
Marcus Garvey, his dream of a free Africa we may
      embrace.
But Africa's independence has been hijacked
Economic independence you see not
Young men and women you need!
That your people economically you would free!

For a daylong, I look for a Redeemer
A Saviour I seek
To loose me from the shackles of death and oppression
That with joy my soul may leap once again
With the joy, I had when independence I was told was
      granted
A free land I was to be again, so I had thought
What a celebration that was!

Alas!
An illusion it became!
Goodwill among your leaders lacking
Elite leaders to say "Enough!"
Leaders who would declare,
"From today, $1 US dollar will be equivalent to $1
      African dollar!"
A first step to set yourself free from slavery and bondage
      by design.
A goodwill you desperately are in need of.

My bones have been crashed
But they still yearn to find strength again
And the peace that for centuries I have known not
That it may return to me
An answered prayer
of those whose souls anguished
and in prayer agonized for my children
For my Redeemer lives!
Yes, I know he lives!
He shall deliver us once and for all!

In cold blood your senior statesman is murdered!
From lands afar come henchmen and accomplices
to his death!
With powerful weapons of mass destruction
on defenceless Libya, they descend!
For laws, they pass to stop others
That in their arsenals weapons of mass destruction
they may not stock
So, an easy battle for them would be
Minimal casualties for him and countless for you!
While hopeless, helpless, and defenceless
the weak will remain
And in shame Africa hopelessly watched!

A cooperating senior statesman of Africa
to the sword he is put!
Plans of a united Africa with him to the grave go
Plans of a developed Libya and Africa to thwart!
A common threat of an awakened giant to stop!
Her sons and daughters, signs of threat not to read!
None of her leaders condemn Western bourgeoisie!

Disguised as "Freedom propagation!"
But ingenuity, independence and African development
    killing it is!
None of the African nations
Gaddafi had helped with massive investments
raises a voice at the advancing army
And in shame Africa hopelessly watched!

Against a flea from afar they come!
"He killed his people" a common fallacy they cry!
A selective justice to carry out!
Others who killed your people (Africa) from his land
    not to bother!
Who grants you permission to destroy my land?
Your assembly of the few always the fate of others to
    decide!
Whose agenda is always skewed to your wants and
    needs!
With a so-called "International Community" – your
    community tag attached!
Carefully crafted to win acceptance to justify
    annihilation of the weak and defenceless
    inhabitants of the globe
And in shame Africa hopelessly watched!

I bemoan you my son!
None of your statesmen but Mugabe condemns this
    aggression
None of them challenges the insurgents and their
    backers!
A weakness you display that may cause your downfall!
Congo DR, a catastrophe engineered!

Millions fallen and none intervenes!
Rwanda, Uganda beneficiaries to evil backed by evil men
Yet none so-called "International Community" is
    moved!
For my wealthy, they are after and not lasting peace they
    seek
And my blind leaders see it not!
None to speak back!
Gaddafi, we mourn you!
And in shame Africa hopelessly watched!

Nigeria – Abuja from scratch to build!
$2 billion, a loan IMF offers
The usual "credit card" debt
Developing countries with usury to trap
Usury they conjure up
An endless debt not meant to be paid back
they conjure up!
Nigeria, my sometimes-weird child
$2 billion in cash she offers that her IMF debt be paid
    in full!
But IMF cash not to accept!
"Not in our interest to accept Nigerian cash!"
IMF through clenched teeth seem to be saying
An obvert sign that it is not to "help"
but to milk the cow they are there for!

And in debt Nigeria, like the rest is trapped!
Trapped in a worldwide cobweb of financial blackmail
Of an international capital
A lesson Africa to learn she must

Then in Dr. Ngozi Iwuoha one of Africa's educated
women
Nigeria finds rescue
For Mother Africa had to bring forth one of her
brightest daughters
A genius of a woman
That through her ingenuity and tact
Nigeria's debt to IMF would pay
That her country from perpetual debt of the IMF she
would free!
For no country that ever got IMF/World Bank loan
offer
Ever stayed the same!
A perpetual credit card debt they incurred
Never to be the same again!
And let all Africa shout: "Hear! Hear! Hear!"

A bridge you desire to build
A loan quickly offered by the lending institutions
A goodwill gesture earnestly given
But "Only a reputable company"
from the lending institution's home country
a contract to be given"
That your bridge they may build
Their bidding price is the most expensive, you sigh and
refuse!
Twice the cost, compared to other bidders!
"Then the loan not to come!" So, they say.
But the bridge you desperately need, so you oblige
And money returns to their country
A loan you still have to repay!
A win-win master for the lender it is!

A game, craftily planned
A game craftily executed by so-called G8 (G7) or G20!

And so economic liberators
All developing nations must seek
If to be free, indeed, they are to
For there in offices of marble they meet
Cigar after cigar in their hands
A master plan not to be botched they come up with
Nations of the world – the poor to enslave
And the learned in developing countries not to see
Many bought, that their countries they may help to sell!
And few Mugabes, few Gaddafis to see –
Economic liberators and Africa misses them!

Mugabe is a "dictator"
Museveni is not!
Laurent Kabila is a "dictator"
Mobutu is not!
Gaddafi is a "dictator"
Mubarak is not!
Laurent Gbagbo is a "dictator"
Kagame is not!
A Western tale that defies my African logic
Fate, always making me to believe his story as genuine
        history
While my historians to sleep they go
Nothing to say, nothing to write and nothing to correct!

CHAPTER 20

TRUST BREACHED, DIFFICULT TO BE TRUSTED AGAIN!

That your children were deliberately infected with
     syphilis
and not treated for decades
Arouses fear and suspicion again!
How cruel your fellow man can be
You are reminded
That a guinea pig you were made to be
As the course of the disease in you he observed
The cruelty of your fellow man.

Should someone kill a dog
A case of cruelty to animals
will be charged against him, in his land
Should someone starve his pet
A case of being heartless to a creature
will be slapped upon him
And behind bars he will find himself!

But for you, fine it is!
When someone kills you, or harms you
For man, you are not!
Neither an animal you are!
At least in the eyes of your friend!

The syphilis study was uncovered
Your people purposely infected with syphilis in his land
A natural progression of the disease left to take its course
Left to develop a general paralysis of the insane
and other complications!
While their stone hearts no guilt they carried!

Ever wondered how many other studies
that never reached your ears were and are done?
How many you have not seen?
Could you trust all gifts you were given?
Well, this, your sons and daughters wonder!

Guatemala STD study:
American government an official apology they now offer!
That a wrong deed it was
Against an unsuspecting people
Infected with syphilis, gonorrhoea and other STDs in
        the 1940s
But conscience to the dog they had thrown
Should this apology be accepted?
Should it be accompanied by restitution?

I have no time to mention your Congo DR
Vaccination Programme!
A Programme against polio
An experiment Programme unauthorized?
And the world is hushed
That questions mustn't be asked
An introduction of disease from the wild
On you and you know it not!

Unfortunately, no disease to introduce
Can remain in you alone
An escape into the environment the disease would
And a pandemic soon to be
Mankind not to contain
No secret to keep
No cure to be found.

2020, "Another new disease's arrival" is announced!
It is called "Coronavirus!" "Covid-19," they term it!
"From China, it is," so they claim!
It reaches every corner of the globe!
"A pandemic," they call it! Nearly every country in the
        world is affected!
Another creation of an out-of-control scheme
To inhabitants of the earth, fear to induce
Impending schemes of "Vaccine to All" in waiting!
With chips to be inserted!

Unknown to many are the constituents of the vaccines
        to come!
An "impending" mark of the beast to be?
That no one without the mark would be allowed to buy
        or sell?
A subtle opportunity and need for selling of vaccines
        amplified!
A movie of 2003 had already "predicted" Coronavirus
        disease!
"hydroxychloroquine" medication for the ailment,
the movie had suggested!
17 years before the pandemic came out of "Wuhan,
        China!"

And you still trust them?

Time for Africa, "Covid-20" to create!
Like their counterparts, biological weapons to make!
A programme you need
That none of the bullies would scorn at you nor bully you!
For your arsenals a stockpile, you too shall have
A time to unleash it in peace time, you too to do!
And watch if some animals who are more equal than
      others wouldn't come!
If they wouldn't come to emasculate you! ("To smoke
      you out the holes!" George Bush)
For causing of death of thousands they would blame you
      of!
Yet none has even come out in the open to tell them
"Thou art the one! The causer of the troubles of the
      world!"
Thousands of lives sacrificed worldwide at the altar of
      mammon.
European Union is silent
And so is Russia!
None is there to call out the bullies!

A fool surely man is!
Science and scientists
implications of engineered viruses not to see!
An escape into the environment overlooked
To one "species" of a people
perhaps they thought it were to be confined
Escape to all "species" alas they have!
This, they never saw!
For in the image of God we all were created

A common ancestry we share
And mingling we shall!
An overlooked truth
And the Creator, at man laughs!

For when a people you sterilize against their will
Their women, their pride you take away
Thousands of my women raped by their captors during
    slavery!
Their men you humiliate
A Programme of intent crafted in the corridors of
    Washington
And pursued by "Scientists" and law enforcement
    officers
But unabated by the law makers
Then Africa, you wonder, when suspicious she remains
For these injustices, we still remember!

"For to wage war you need guidance"[42] (NIV Study
    Bible Proverbs 24:6).
"In the multitude of counsel lies safety"[43] (Proverbs
    11:14 KJV).
So, kings and leaders, advice they require
Unadulterated counsel they need
To fail to heed to correction is folly
For power often blinds
To many, absolute power corrupts
Sense not to see
Safety not to perceive
Embroidered in your own world of lunacy
A god you think you are
Into Iraq on flimsy and unfounded rationale goes Bush

And on the same flimsy grounds his successor
into Libya goes Obama
Innocent people to kill
To the voice of reason never to listen.
Engrossed in their own world of lunacy
That their countrymen they may show
"Tough leaders" they are
But fools in the eyes of our Maker and the world they are!

A voice of reason is ignored
Decisions made in haste
To war you desire to go
No other voices, no other reason to hear
Millions to slaughter
Child left with no father, no mother
Mother left with no child, no husband
Pain and sorrow to inflict for a lifetime
Consideration for your fellow man you chose not
A lifelong story you left
Unmindful of the calamity you left behind.

A god you thought you were
And suddenly destruction soon to overtake you
A price paid for your stupidity
For wisdom, you thought you had
Only through your own eyes you chose to see
But a wider view and understanding you perceived not
And a fool you were.

It is a Western bourgeoisie
A Western pride and arrogance
That seeks to dominate and impoverish

A culture of conquering, dividing, and ruling
A hegemonic influence sown across the globe
And a sharp memory we lack not
For a friend and foe, we can know
A genuine friend who empathizes for the weak
and oppressed we now can tell and know.

Who sacrifices to share with those in sorrow?
Those who suffer at the hands of the rich,
the powerful and strong?
At the hands of those who exploit the widow
and the defenceless
And to their cries they heed not
A real friend full of empathy, Africa does indeed know
      her!

"For their fate and destiny is not our plight,"
So, they say.
"Their worry and misery are of their own-making,"
So, they mock.
"A self-inflicted and self-afflicted destiny
And a product of lack of ingenuity and purpose
That a cause for concern we see not
But an opportunity to enrich ourselves we see
For in disorder and chaos enormous profit margins we see
And there to go we choose
In destabilized and unruly states
Business opportunity we see
While busy at one another they rise up against
Their profit to slash
Ours to increase
And in luxury we are to live!"

Excess power some hold
Excess authority they still press for
That with it they may oppress
and rule the weak and defenceless
Power, excess power corrupts
Turning a blind eye to oppression
and suffering of the defenceless
Ever wondered why only them hold power in the UN?
Democracy – a fallacy
Absolute power to veto the voice of reason
Other nations' voices not to hear!
And "democratic" they claim to be!
And in lunacy with zeal, democracy they want to export!

Yet those who seek for power among us
Their wings we chop
Power, sweet power not to be shared!
For if all got power,
Where then shall the vanquished be found?
"A classless society," – a fallacy.
A dream never to be realized
A utopia world not to see!
A dream conceived to wreck profiteering and dominance
A dream never to be courted
A dream never to be entertained!

Religion, land, and food
Human needs, conflicts to bring
Land, shelter, and food
Basic human needs, conflicts to induce
In search of comfort and peace
That in leisure they may live

"Religion," their spiritual connection to their creator
they may find
For spiritual beings, we all are
But to kill to advance our religion, our faith we detest
For with love, Christ, his "religion" or faith to advance
Not with sword Peter he told
"For those who kill by the sword
By the sword they will die,"[44] (NIV Study Bible.
        Matthew 26:52; John 18:11).

Love, the purest "religion" of them all
Both friend and foe to love
"Love," the Creator's name
Above ethnicity, religion, and politics love is
Love, his call to advance
Religiously and passionately
Your enemy and foe not to kill
But to win through love.

To dominate and subdue the earth
A command he gave us
To dominate and subdue our fellow man
he detests
This, we must live for, this we must aspire for.
Food, we all need
For hunger dehumanizes us
Strife to fuel
Pain too hard to bear.

How can you find happiness
when your neighbour in poverty he wallows?
How can you rejoice

when your friend has nothing to eat?
Discontentment and disillusionment hunger breeds
"For when nothing your enemy has, feed him,"[45] (NIV
    Study Bible Matthew 5:43-44, Romans 12:20.).
The Prophet's teaching to fulfil
Unnecessary wars to vanquish
Fuelled out of selfishness and hatred
That those who look different from us
Or speak differently
Our enemies they are, we think
An erroneous belief, Satan's trap.

Botswana once a partner, now they debunk
A war of words they pick up against her!
That a path to clothe and humanize her Bushmen
she has chosen
A path to a better Botswana not to take!
So, she is ordered by the "lords" who know it all
For a very lucrative business she will kill!
"Kalahari tours" to destroy!
For Africans never wondered why "Kalahari tours"
take place yearly!
"Tour Competitions" in the deep jungle and desert
heart of Africa, held!
For there, the Bushman who carries diamonds with them
on their almost naked bodies live!
There, a lucrative business
for my "deeply concerned friend of the Bushman affairs"
    thrives!

A relocation of my poor, naked, uneducated,
nomad child of Africa

A decent home built by the Tswana government
That school he may get, raises eyebrows
and protests in London!
"That the government never cares for the Bushman,"
they wail!
Survival International, parades my naked people in
        London!
Flying them to London, a protest arranged!
A guise of a people whose hearts are not genuine
No true care they have for the Bushman!
And no genuine care they have for Africa!

A loss of free acquisition of my diamonds they see!
A business shut down on them by development!
For how could a relocation of a people to modern
        houses
be viewed as tyranny of a government?
How could dressing of a people in the 21st century
be seen as a retrogressive move of a government?
How would empowering of a people who
had had no basic amenities for centuries
be taken as a violation of "human rights" by a
        government?

My shame is my enemy's joy
My ignorance and shame, my enemy's opportunity
to make money
My nakedness, his laughingstock and joy
My images to shoot and parade across the globe
to his joy
Hidden in it, a lucrative business of my precious stones
And my Mother, asleep never to wonder why

Africa's development, they violently resist!
But our wealth we shall not for a song give away
Our self-empowering policy for free we shall not trade
For determined to develop our people and nation we are!
And our shame shall cease to be a profit for you!

The Bushman, they parade on a box
His shameful fate they display
The Masai, they parade on a box
Numerous books in publication
His pierced body to display
A lucrative adventurous business for them to have
Relocation of a people by my government, foreigners
    resist!
Those from a distant land "lobby" for my people!
Lobbying for a people in a land not their own!

They resist on behalf of a people who never said, "No!"
But on behalf of a people whose business
they foresee being curtailed,
they lobby!
Their hope of making "cool" money
from diamonds to vanish
So, they are to instruct my government not to relocate
    her people!
Defiance would imply, "No aid from us!"

When was the last time
you ever told them what to do?
When was the last time
you told them how they were to govern?
Did they ever listen to you

when you told them homosexuality is sinful?
It is a curse in my land, an unwelcome deed?
No! Your aid Uganda, you lost!
They didn't listen to you Zimbabwe!

Why then do they have solutions for you, O Africa?
Solutions not in your interest!
Solutions for someone else's interest!
And some of your leaders, their stance they change!
Never, do so O Africa!
For now, you need to grow up!
That your affairs you may direct!

I heard my teacher in New England lament
That to keep New England backward and dependent
Establishment of industries was not to be done!
That backward New England was to be kept
A territory for raw materials' procurement it was to be
Finished goods New England was to receive
The English decree to keep her under perpetual bondage!
A similar creed exercised on mother Africa for centuries!
A "blank check" New England was given for her
        industries
That goods may now be produced
And land to remain underdeveloped
A path and only route towards her independence
lay in severing relations with her master in England
That "Enough" Great Britain was to be told!
England, never again to dominate
Their own industries now to build
A will power of a people
Sustained by a determined will power

For trust had now been eroded
England not to trust again
A lesson mother Africa you think has not learned from?

Once, I pondered deeply at my form!
I pondered at my ways!
I found man was the same,
regardless of ethnicity, creed or colour!
I also examined closely what I am often portrayed
in my land as being like
I discovered that the same traits were also present in his
    land!
I was made to believe wrong was only found in me!
This, I came to realize was not true!

"Corruption" I have, "networking" they do!
"Nepotism" I have, "it depends on who you know" they
    have!
"Bribery" I have, "tipping" they do!
"Injustice" I have, "vetoing" they do!
"Looting" I have, "looking for food" they do! [46]
    (Zenovia, B. on Kanye West, 2006).
"Deals" I have, "business transactions" they do!
My trust wavered a little as I pondered on the above
But Africa understands!
She knows that mankind is the same!

CHAPTER 21

FROM HISTORY AND NATURE, INHABITANTS OF THE EARTH NOT TO LEARN!

Berlin, O Berlin!
Once, a divided city you were!
Partitioned to separate a people!
Ideology at the core of battle
You, the city that partitioned mother Africa
Separating family, clan, and friendship
A common heritage taken away
A wedge of animosity planted
The same experience now you dreaded!
An end to the siege you called for
The wall of separation to tear down
Would you now to Africa turn?
Her walls too that they may crumble down?

Forests, insulted
God's canopy destroyed
Chemicals on environments, unleashed
Contamination of high proportion unfathomed
Secrets to life, God's power, unlocked
Mankind; hidden and encased secrets of life to alter

Seeds marvel and mourn,
Animals wonder and cry
Humans in awe lament
"Carcinogens!" the earth sighs
"Creation" engineered!
Cancer multiplies
To power, sweet, power man to hold
Nature insulted, and to learn from it, man refuses!

In fury nature cries out
Violently she protests
At the way earthlings have treated her
Protection she was to have
Nurtured she was to be
But the rich and the affluent had pummelled on her
Chernobyl, a desolate place
Hiroshima and Nagasaki
An agony of the environment and mankind
Oceans disturbed
The foundations of the earth destroyed
Underground and undersea atomic bombs to test.

The foundations of the earth rumble
In agony, they cry
But none hears of it
Not even one cares
That to the earth's aid they may come
The earth's tectonic plates shaken
And not one shouts for a stop!
For to dominate – man desires
A new way to wipe out fellow man he looks for.

In anger, Indian Ocean Tsunami rolls
273,000 lives to claim[47] (Joseph Grant Swank, Mar, 2005).
In bitterness Katrina, the hurricane fumes
1,836 lives to take
In vengeance Haiti earthquake rumbles
316, 000 lives to gore
Hurricane waters plummet inhabitants of the land
Waves and waters overstepping their boundaries
Property and lives to claim
In rage Japan is swallowed
Nuclear contamination again to sea and land to see
The earthquake and Tsunami too strong to stop
Technology not to abate the creator's wrath
Nor the enemy's desire to annihilate earthlings.

The mountains of the earth quake
Their fury foundations hot lava to unleash
Volcanic ash to spit
Soot to the sky rises
No planes to fly
Earthquake after earthquake
And hurricane after hurricane
Thousands of lives to annihilate
And earthlings ask not
as to why the fury is turned on them
For a few have had had
The foundations of the earth disturbed
And in rage nature fumes
not to be tamed.

New Zealand cries
Australia mourns

Chile weeps
Congo DR fumes and so does China
America in record floods and record twisters, sighs
In turmoil, the earth is
And mankind asks not why it is so
From her Maker, all have turned away
Each seeks his own way and will
To her Maker not to return
Violence fills the earth
As with supersonic machines made by hands of men
Mankind wipes out one another
And spilled blood from the earth cries for vengeance to
　　　God
But mankind still busy he is
Other lives to snap off
And the voice of God she hears not.

Will mankind ponder through his dealings with his God?
Will he reflect on how his neighbour he has mistreated?
Will he think through how he has violated nature?
Land, sea, and sky he was given to take care of
Will he quickly see that his stewardship
leaves much to be desired?
Will he ask for forgiveness from his creator?
Will he to his neighbour go and ask for amends to be
　　　made?
Will he revisit nature and be a good steward?

No! He seems uncaring and fixated
in his own world of luxury, lunacy and riches
His God, forgotten
To his neighbour, still plotting ill

And testing fetishes underground and underwater
That superior to his neighbour he may remain
New ways to exterminate his neighbours' life he seeks
Obsessed with temporally and perishable goals
Never to store up his riches in heaven
where moth and rust never devour wealth!

Who will take away this disillusionment
and disappointment from my people?
Who will wipe away this distaste
and desperation from my children?
Who will disperse this discontentment
from my youth?
Who will disassociate this destruction
from mother Africa?

Used and dumped
A lesson too hard to learn and grasp by your leaders
Mobutu Sese Seko, Jonas Savimbi,
Idi Amin, Saddam Hussein, Laurent Kabila,
an endless list.
Used and dumped, an agenda unfathomed
Yet to prostitute themselves
your short-sighted leaders still continue
The enemy not to see
Courting trouble and misery untold
Their "mentally myopicness" and folly not to see
As to the grave they drag with them the innocent
and the unsuspecting.

Your wealth locked up
Your enemy not to blame

Charles Kapungwe

Your foolish undiscerning leaders to fault
For learning from history, they refused
Multiplying the slain and deceived among you
Because from history and nature they had refused to
        learn

"Dissent is not disloyalty!"
My son, King, heralds words of wisdom
"For they have everything to teach others
but nothing to learn from them!"
"Wisdom can be gotten,"
My mother taught me
"From a pebble into an anthill went wisdom"
my mother's words would say
An African saying advising nobles to learn even from the
        young
But to no one, do the world powers listen
And into the abyss they plunge themselves
And all those they lead.

"The know-it-all went with faeces to their in-laws"
so, says an African adage.
Another proverb my mother used to tell me
So that words of wisdom would be inculcated into me
Those, who to advice they could not heed
Their ears blocked to a voice of reason and advice
To the in-laws they went
with something to bring shame to them
Unknown to them that their shame had stuck on them
Their private secret shame to their in-laws to bring
For an assumption and presumption
of "Know it all" they had displayed

272

A warning that they had faeces on them, they could not
    take!
Their shame, therefore, to their in-laws they took
Displayed to those who value them highly
Their respect and honour not to have again!

To those who cared they refused to listen
To those who were genuinely concerned about their
    outlook
they would not listen
Advice unaccepted, advice ignored
With the smell of poop
To the in-laws the man went
A disgrace to the in-laws and to himself he became
Shame never to be erased
For advice, he refused to accept
And folly was his end.

"History often has a tendency
to repeat itself, son,"
as a boy, my father would tell me,
My little mind, his wisdom, not to conceptualize
In curiosity, I tried to envision what he meant
Unaware the future lay in waiting
A mystery unfathomed to unveil
In amazement, today, I understand!

When as a little boy in my father's house
Only 16, and in secondary school
Into Afghanistan rolled the Soviet Union in 1979
"Soviet Intervention in Afghanistan,"
the media dubbed it.

The world led by the U.S. rebuffed the Soviets' adventurism
A sponsored rebellion had them forced out!
A retreat of a might empire to see 10 years later!
A rare retreat by a superpower in contemporary times
A great feat for one ideology against the other.

22 years later the U.S. intervenes in Afghanistan!
"A global war on terror" it is deemed by politicians
My boggled mind to understand it tries
"If it weren't right for the Soviets,
it may not be right for the Americans," it postulates
No, I was wrong!
"Surely, history repeats itself, son!"
The words from a wise father to remember!

Sanctions, sanctions, sanctions!
Sanctions they call on Russia!
"That Ukraine's sovereignty they flouted!"
A fellow superpower to the sword they try to put
Her economy to rot!
"Guilty" is the verdict they pronounce on Russia!
The finger that feeds them, they forget
Europe, gas from her you cherish
America, to the International Space Centre
a ride from them you desire!
A log in your eyes not to see,
A speck in others' eye you desire to remove!
Ukraine unequivocally Russia it is!
And so is Georgia
Russian security to them tied
never their country at risk to put
Afghanistan, Iraq wars, quickly forgotten!

Freedom we cry for
Freedom we fight for
And freedom we defend
The British, the Americans had to resent
That freedom from them the British had withheld
'Till to arms they took .
That "Land of the Free,"
America, they would call
"We hold these truths to be self-evident,
that all men are created equal,
that they are endowed by their Creator
with certain unalienable Rights,
that among these are Life, Liberty
and the pursuit of Happiness,"
said Thomas Jefferson, [48] (Quotes®.net, August 2011).

Now a crisis that your sons
and daughters knew not looms
A crisis of escape from creative suffering
By world powers through years of economic
        strangulation
and exploitation
that food and a better life
beyond your borders they may find
A thing that none should be surprised of but only a fool!
"History repeats itself,"
my father as a young boy had taught me
My learned and wise friends
should have known this a long time ago too!
For indeed, history does repeat itself!

But why should you be accursed

or looked down upon?
For to look for greener pastures is in man
A first not for you to do so
Nor the last will you ever be
Not the first to go afar, a better life to find
Millions you saw for the "Scramble for Africa"
Europeans in Africa to resettle
Thousands North America saw
Freedoms to seek
A better life to find
From Asia to lands afar they went
From Mexico to U.S. they come
A common story of every inhabitant of the earth
Nothing too extraordinary to have you surprised!

That honey in the wilderness,
your children too need to find
a cause for concern for them it should not be
For if to peruse through history they chose
The annals of life history they check
There, written are survival instincts of humanity
To places far and beyond they went
Looking for a better life
Food and shelter they may find
Riches to find
The strong to survive and the weak they killed
And a new land they inherited!

An outcry now I hear!
Xenophobic are people of the land!
Europe detests Africans!
Paris and London jobs not to give

Forgotten that to their lands they went
African wealth to share or pilfer!
"Fenced in" Europe announces!
In U.S. too, in cages immigrants to be put!
Even Israel, "Niggers" in rage they call you!
As they shut doors in your face that you may not enter
    or stay
History, quickly forgotten
That none had "fenced them in!"
Instead, many (natives) were displaced in their land or
    killed!
Native Americans, Aborigines, the Africans!
History never to recall!
And the learned deeply sigh!

America, (a few) detests the immigrants!
"Why do they come here?" they ask.
"Poor fellows!" a stupid question they ask.
Annals of history never to read
The right question should have been
"Why did our fathers come here?"
Better still they could have asked,
"Why did our fathers go to Africa
and what are our kin still doing there?"
Let them live!

South Africa a shame too!
Years of anguish and pain quickly forgotten!
Your neighbours harboured you in time of need
That your land you may enjoy
Their land your land had become
But quickly you have forgotten

Your pain and sorrow once caused by settlers forgotten!
With tires your kin you burn
And no conscience pricks you!
Put on sackcloth and repent to your God and your
     Maker
For a curse, you court
God have mercy on us
for this gross sin, we have committed
against our brothers and sisters
For from history, we too refused to learn.

CHAPTER 22

AND TO WAR TO
FREE THEMSELVES
THEY WENT!

From its mouth, the lion,
carcasses it could not release
that the hyena could feed
On and on the lion held onto the carcass,
the hyena to starve
Until to the bush the hyena went
and "Gorillas" they became!
Guerrilla warfare to launch
That carcasses they may get and eat!
From the stingy lion's mouth!
With wild animals, they were numbered
To the bush they went
In the bush, they slept
And on snakes they crawled
For "gorillas," they had become
That carcasses they may eat!

United National Independence Party (UNIP) and "Cha
    Cha Cha," Zambia created!
African National Congress (ANC) and "Umkhonto we
    Sizwe," South Africa invented!
South West Africa People's Organization (SWAPO),
    Namibia brought forth!

Zimbabwe African People's Union (ZAPU) and
Zimbabwe African National Union (ZANU), roared
     Zimbabwean "gorillas!"
Zimbabwe People's Revolutionary Army (ZIPRA) they
     shouted!
Mozambique Liberation Front ("FRELIMO" – from the
     Portuguese *Frente de Libertação de Moçambique*)
     said Mozambique!
Union for Total Independence of Angola, (UNITA) and
Popular Liberation Movement (MPLA) cried Angola!
Tanganyika African National Union (TANU)
     proclaimed Tanzania!
Kenya African National Union (KAU) and "Mau Mau,"
     announced Kenya!
As one by one
"Gorillas" to the street and to the bush they took.
For "gorillas," they had become
and guerrilla warfare to sustain
Aware that there were no carcasses from the stingy lion
     for them to eat
No, not one, without a fight!

And so, blood was spilled
Spilled for Mother Africa
"Africa, My Africa,"
Mpundu Mutale, Zambia's freedom fighter
in a song, laments[53] (Africa, my Africa)
For in numbers you died
Died at the hands of your master
No carcasses to be given freely, you had learned
No, not one, without a fight
No oppressor gives carcasses freely

From history, this you learned
The British, America fought that she could be "free!"
Africa too to be free, she had to fight
Cruelty and savagery but a reasonable stance and cause
    to take
A right cause for justice to prevail.

"Communists" freedom fighters are branded by
    capitalists!
"Capitalists" freedom fighters are called by communists!
For when you dared the capitalists' injustices,
"a communist" you became
Even though to the East clearly ties you never had
And when you dared the communists' injustices,
"a capitalist" you became
Even though to the West clearly ties you never had!

To the core of their hearts they believed
To the core of their innermost being they were convinced
That a more and just society was one which valued justice
and freedom
A society that valued human dignity and respect
for one another
A society that valued the rule of law
And a society that believed and upheld a constitution
The constitution that treated and recognized all men as
    equal
And as partners in development.

For from tyrants in Europe they ran
From oppression and injustice, they left
A more free and just society to establish

To America they came
"A land of the free and the brave,"
they deemed it.
but from tyrants they could not run
for in the heart of man lay tyrants.
When a promise of, "All men are born equal,"
enacted on a piece of paper which they could not uphold,
more blood had to be shed!
And the land was once again stained
The cries of those who were not free before their Maker
    arose
For the colour of their skin had imprisoned them
to inequality.

For from tyrants they ran
from oppression and injustice, they left
a more free and just society to establish
To Africa they came
To the land of freedom and peace
But from tyrants they could not run
For in the heart of man lay tyrants
When a promise of "A protectorate of the land"
was fashioned
With blood the land was stained
Of those sold to toil in distant lands
And those killed trying to free themselves
For "communists" they were!

And the world was silent
When in large numbers they died
An unarmed and defenceless people died
At the hands of trigger-happy soldiers and police, they died

A voice of anguish and pain, they were trying to
    extinguish
Motionless and lifeless down the school boys and girls lay
Their lives exterminated by the bullet of oppression
Life and hope sucked out
Fear and intimidation to grip
"Freedom is coming tomorrow,"
again, that they may not shout,
"Get ready mama prepare for your freedom," [26] (Sarafina
    – Whoopi Goldberg, 1992).
Soweto school boys and girls told to shut up.
That refrain, never to utter again, they are ordered.

An echo of mourning and wailing
is heard in the Drakensberg Mountains
Sorrow and sighing are heard in Soweto
Mothers and fathers, their children never to see again!
Elsewhere, orphans and widows increase
Freedom fighters to the ground lay
Misery and hopelessness aroused
That hate may induce hate
A cycle unbroken
And your leader Nelson Mandela not to see
Your leader Walter Sisulu not to hear from
Oliver Tambo, in exile, not to see too
And in silence the world watches!

And the world was silent
As in large numbers they died
Thousands the field claimed
Thousands the river claimed
As in Matabeleland, Mashonaland and beyond they died

In "Orange Free State" you lived,
but free you were not!
Slaves in your own country of birth you were made to be!
Like wild animals you were hunted beyond your borders
Oh Rhodesia!
For freedom, you desired
But freedom you could not be granted
When you politely asked for it
None was willing to listen to the voice of reason
A demand not to pay attention to!

And so, to the bush you went Robert Mugabe
Yes, to the bush Joshua Nkomo you took
To the bush Sam Nujoma, Samora Machel you went
But even there you were hunted for
That your life they would take
Memories easily forgotten
As pressure on you now is given
that the basket of the fruit now you may share
A large portion to them to belong once again!
Your independence, their independence to be
Benefits either way to them to roll
Memories easily forgotten!

And in silence the world watched
While in large numbers you died
In the fields of Mozambique, you fell
In the deserts of Namibia and Algeria you were cut away
In the forests of Northern Rhodesia, Angola,
Congo, Tanganyika, Nyasaland, Kenya you fell
Yes, in the forests of Ghana, Uganda
From the living you were cut away

Nigeria, a cry in the delta is heard.
And the world in silence watched
Now the world can cry
At the "mistreatment of his people!"

"Mugabe's people are hungry,"
Now the "world cries!"
Now the pain they feel for you, "Mugabe's people!"
That democracy you now may have
Democracy the world had cared less about before
A paradox of care and love!
Now the silence has been broken
Interest of the people at their hearts they have!
Now Africa wonders and is perplexed
As to why now so much concern and care
have been aroused!

It is a paradox of a tale
A riddle unfathomed
That world leaders (including Bill Clinton)
In London would gather
Mandela's 90th birthday to celebrate
this June 26, 2008
A man once dubbed a "terrorist"
His birthday to celebrate!
It defies Africa's logic
Her understanding in confusion is left
That the world on a "terrorist"
a Nobel peace prize could be conferred
Logic and understanding defied!

Didn't your conscience burn within you?

Or was it seared as it were, with a hot iron?
When at the expense of a people you called "slaves"
You enriched yourselves?
When at the suffering, toil and labour of them
you fed and clothed yourselves?
When sugar Jamaica gave to you
When cotton and corn the plantations of the South gave
    to you
When from the sweat and anguish of families came your
    comfort?
Their misery and cry untold
While your conscience remained unmoved?

Didn't your conscience cringe?
When overboard you threw them
Into the unforgiving and unquenchable appetite of the
    deep sea
When to lighten your battered boats by winds and waves
    out you threw them?
While on a long trek of evil you proceeded?
Incidents and episodes of your cruelty
Into your subconscious-self you pushed
Memories too graphic, too gross to remember
A glass of wine to sip, to forget
As another, someone's son or daughter
Someone's father or mother
Is forever taken away from them.

Didn't your conscience flinch?
When with wild animals their sick bodies you left
In the unforgiving terrain of the forests you left them
Their weight unbearable

A cargo too heavy for you to carry
A lost good price a loss of income for you
And so, in the jungle among the wild beasts
you left their dying bodies
And your conscience indeed detached it was!

Didn't your conscience get pricked?
When in the field you made them to work from sunrise
      to sunset?
With little or no pay?
Didn't your conscience shy away?
When one with the other you made them to fight?
As they bruised one another
An entertainment and fun it was
Your possessions and objects they were
And in silence at one another they looked
Knowing that they would be free one day!

The Kenyan uprising, a demand for freedom and
      independence was greeted by ostracization and
      persecution!
The Kenyan demand for independence, deemed *Mau Mau*
was greeted by women raped via use of bottles and men
      castrated via use of pliers
by the British!
The Israelites' massacre by Hitler has been deemed "The
      Holocaust!"
The Africans' displacement from their home en
      masse via the Triangular Slave Trade, massacre
      and genocide via mass incarcerations, medical
      genocide, lynching, police brutality and homicide

in "The Free World" has never been termed "The
Genocide!"

A pass the British are given!
And so are the Americans!
At the Hague not to appear
Native Americans' extermination – a free pass
    executioners receive!
A demand we make today!
That all meaningful African nations from the Hague a
    pull out must be made!
For an unjust court it is!
A court crafted for the poor and for you!
For today (2020), in mockery an African seat to Kenya
    is given on Security Council!
To represent 54 African nations – an experiment that
    will take 54 years for each African country to take
    turns to sit on the Destabilization Council of the
    Wicked
The Council of "Democracy" with powers to veto vested
    in a few!
And Africa laughs!

When love you sow, love you reap
When hate you sow, hatred you reap
For blind are nations and blind are the leaders of the world
To spread love by the sword they see
Bloodshed never friends to win
Friends never to make
Foes and enemies the sword to make
Division and turmoil the sword to plant
Sons of men fail to foresee

Love that covers a multitude of sin
Not to see.

And to death multitudes they lead
To wage wars of persons who desire warring
While in their palaces they remain
Their children not to send
Increasing the slain
Widows and orphans to multiply
And none can stop your myopic leaders
Death and dying of their enemies
Their joy to keep.

The Son of Man preached love for your neighbour,
and he was killed
Martin Luther King, Jr., propounded tolerance
and giving of the other cheek,
he was slain
Malcolm X propagated a philosophy of retaliation
to one who does you wrong
he too was annihilated.

With confusion, your sons and daughters wonder
Which doctrine to choose, they ponder.
That the best and right they may espouse
For fate and death encompass them both
A way forward with soot is clouded
As your leaders, you fail to trail!
That which of their teachings you may embrace!

Only to stop injustice and oppression
did Africa to war go

Charles Kapungwe

A voice of reason today says,
"No war Africa to wage against her oppressors
by way of the barrel of the gun!"

Africa, her carnage of rising up
one against another soon to stop
My brother and sister, enemies they are not
A voice of disunity now never to listen to
A wedge of enmity pushed between us,
that brother against brother we may fight
A cry and pledge to our God we make today
That brotherly love we would spread
and war not to study no more!

CHAPTER 23
THROUGH KILLING – IDEOLOGY TO ADVANCE AND PRESERVE!

Ideology, ideology!
Has the East been delivered?
Has it been delivered from its belief?
For in its name they killed
Enemies eliminated, ideology to keep
and ideology to preserve
"Communists" you were called
Loathed by many that "free speech"
you took away, so they said.
Opposition you denied and sent them to jail
So, you were accused of
And "Capitalists" you deemed them!

Ideology, ideology!
Will the West be delivered?
Delivered from its belief?
For in its name they killed
Enemies eliminated, ideology to keep
and ideology to preserve
"Capitalists" you were called.
Loathed by many that "the poor you trampled upon."
Their freedoms you took away, so they said.

Opposition you denied and sent them to jail
So, you were accused of
And "Communists" you deemed them!

Ideology, ideology!
Has Islam been delivered?
Delivered from its belief?
For in its name they kill
Enemies eliminated, ideology or religion to keep
and ideology to preserve
"Jihadists" you call yourselves.
Loathed by many that "freedoms"
you take away, so they say.
Other faiths denied, sent them to jail or killed
So, you are accused of and you confess to the same
"Infidels" never permitted to live!
Islam: Convert or perish!

At the hands of Jihadists
Sudan's males' blood to spill
An inheritance denied
A threat from their neighbour
Not permitted to live
At the hands of ideologists, the boys fall
Young lives the deserts claim
The forests the slain not to count
Southern Sudan's males to kill
Darfur by the sword or barrel of a gun to devour
and through rape to rip off.

At the hands of extremists,
women wail

Their bodies defiled
And leaders nothing to say
No charges filed
Ethnic cleansing in progress
and Islam not to stop
innocent people put to death
Darfur, the agony you bring
Mother Africa cries
The slain never to count.

At the hands of extremists,
women wail
Their loved ones in cold blood massacred
And leaders nothing to say
No charges filed
Ethnic cleansing in progress
and Islam not to stop
innocent people put to death
For to Northern Nigeria the Southerners went
"Christians" they were deemed
From their buses, out they were ordered
All but the driver in cold blood they are exterminated
Islam to defend
A heartless misguided people
Their ideology to advance
And mother Africa cries
The slain never to count.

Judaism, the forerunner to Christianity
Israel grafted by God to show His plan
for the world
Surrounded by hostile nations, Israel constantly

under threat
But only by the hand of God she is expected to survive
To war they go that hostile nations they may defeat
Their existence to establish
Her complete obliteration they seek
Enemies of our soul, Satan we may see
Alas! Wicked man Satan never to see!

But when lessons Israel fail to learn
That a Saviour in Jesus God provides
That to war they may go no more
Hostilities from neighbours to arise
A thorn in their flesh to remain
And to war constantly Israel must go
Her existence to protect
And her faith to defend.

Christians, true Christians ideology not to uplift
That through it they may conquer
Those who fight and conquer by the sword
By the sword they will go
Christ not to represent
Their ideology to present
Christians owe no man anything but love
For their God is love
That all men with Christ may live
In the present life and beyond
Ideology not to spread but faith.

Christians the world lacks
For to war men and women not to go
An ideology not by force to impose

But all men to love as Christ so commanded them
Knowledge of their Creator to all men to bring
"Crusaders" erroneously the world calls them!
"Zionists" the world deems them!
Lovers of mankind true believers are
The word of their Master to honour
Spreading the tidings of peace
at home and abroad
Reconciling man to his Creator
And man, to fellow man
Their faith not by force to spread
Yes, true Christians
A born again experience to cherish!
And the word of God, true Christians
to all mankind to preach.

CHAPTER 24
THE WEST AND THE EAST: YOUR GOODNESS WE CHERISH!

We applaud America for her humanitarian aid
reaching out to nations under distress
Her missionaries serving and saving the world
From evil, they rescue
America at her best that the state may pursue
The core of American values which others have corrupted
Following their selfishness, good values abandoned
American sacrifice to rediscover once again.

We applaud America "The Lost Boys" of Sudan they rescue
From tyrants and anarchists, she retrieves
Sufferings too numerous, too unbearable to count
But America remembers her true values
From the jaws of marauding lions
the boys are rescued
From the pit of hell, they are brought forth.

America, you who the hungry have fed,
we praise.
That your duties to the world not to neglect
Suffering and pain you know
From the Civil War to the Great Depression
From World Wars to segregation

Lessons too deep inculcated
Lessons too obvert to forget
Experience to learn from
And lessons to teach and share
That the world, a better place it may be.

America, we applaud you
That the Somali Bantu you resettle
A people displaced
A people unaccepted
By autocratic and repressive regimes
For ethnicity and language, stumbling blocks
to them they became
Erroneously, we had scolded at you
That skin colour you had judged
A people from a distant land you had mistreated
But evil is in every heart we now have learned
And the sins of her forefathers,
the sons and daughters not to give.
Saddam Hussein, his people he mistreated
Adolf Hitler, his people he killed
War crimes fugitive Radovan Karadzic,
his kinsmen he exterminated
And so, did Charles Taylor, Gnassingbe Eyadema,
and Idi Amin
For in every man, regardless of colour, evil resides.

We applaud you that from every nation
you have gathered them
That in peace and not in pieces, in America they may live
From Eastern Europe, they came
From Ethiopia, you brought them

From Sudan, they were received
From Somalia, refuge they found
And from Rwanda, Burundi, Liberia, Guinea,
Sierra Leone, Togo and Congo DR
rest they were promised
American values reclaimed
For a Land of Refugee, you are
and a Land of Refugee you have been!

America! A nation with countless number of people
showing goodwill to others!
One of the most, if not the leading nation with most
      generous
private citizens there is!
Americans building churches overseas,
we salute you!
Americans helping nations around the globe with the
      Peace Corps volunteers!
Americans, helping fellow Americans at home and abroad!
We applaud you!
Many private citizens, with American values at heart
We cherish!
No other nation on earth to equal, but only America!
America, the beautiful!

Canada we applaud you!
An old friend in ending oppression in North America
Abolitionists you had harboured
Men and women with caring hearts
Slavery to end
Underground Rail Road to Canada from the South it
      reached

Caring for the oppressed and displaced
Burdens seen, burdens lifted from a people
Working with many Americans of the North and South
Whose conscience and love could not be compromised
Lovers of their God and right
Yes, Canada, Africa remembers!

We applaud you France!
For as a son, Ivory Coast you took
Like a baby you protected her
Nursed and nourished her
To vultures never to abandon
For a people, you cared for
A mutual benefit to have and share
Your second home away from home you made
In harmony, together to live
A delight of Africa
Her wealth to share
and her wealth mutually to benefit.

Your European doors to the immigrant you opened
For a common history, you all share
From the 1800s their master you have been
They who served you, their labours enriching you
Although "freedom" they had cried for
Hate they had not harboured
To rule themselves they had desired
Just like all of you had at one time desired
Your own destiny to make for yourselves.

In awe France, we watch!
Your World Cup soccer team amalgamated

France lifts up the 1998 World Cup
with nearly all players of colour!
Another 2018 World Cup victory by France, a near
    replica!
The English and the rest of the world at you they stare
That according to ability you reward every man
By content of character every man you judge
And skin colour not a parameter to be
And France we applaud you!

Your challenges we overlook
For which nation does not have any?
You strive that together you may live
After all a third of the world you ruled
A home for them you create
Just like a home for you they once had created.
However, we appeal to you
Let them be independent!
Let your hands off Africa!
Grant them back freedom and wealth you continue to
    plunder
and coups you continue to plot!
Francophone countries of Africa grieve continuously!

Portugal, we applaud you!
Angola, Mozambique, and Guinea Bissau
once you had resisted!
Never to let go!
Sao Tome, Cape Verde and Senegal, your influence
    heralded!
Now friends and not foes they are
Now to you for guidance they look

That in harmony we may live
No victor and no vanquished
Together, a common destiny we may share.

Great Britain we applaud you
Once a mighty empire that spanned the entire globe
You who conquered the world
Your language spoken everywhere /
Giving the peoples of the world
Peoples of every tongue and language
A medium of communication
Your education an influence to them all
To you we say, "Thank you!"

Great Britain we applaud you!
Now you open up for the peoples
of your former territories
For no true Commonwealth lives
when closed your borders remain
But a leader of nations you are!
Giving room to many
Though your space too small to accommodate
But as a world leader your doors you open
Tony Blair my nurses from abroad he comforts
A true leader who by example he leads.

Spain, we applaud you!
That your doors you open
"A global village we are,"
so, you say.
Others you receive, and millions of their feet you wash
A leader of the world you had been

From Africa to North and South America
Your territories spanned
Your colonies never to throw under the bus
For a leader, you were
And a leader you are!

We applaud you that your language you gave
Spoken across the oceans
Other peoples to accept
For a common destiny, we share
A common history we have
Your love unbroken
Even by bitter years of struggle
That independence they would get
For you knew "Your freedom was inextricably bound to
    their freedom,"[49] (Martin Luther King, Jr., "I have a
    dream," 1963).
For this, Spain we applaud you!

Germany, we applaud you!
An overcomer of a fascist regime you are!
You have not chosen to live in the past
Racial injustice you have denounced!
Choosing to live in harmony with all men
Your bitter years of history in Africa to forget!
Namibia, the past not to remember!
A new page you have opened!
Welcoming the down-trodden and the oppressed!

Lessons too deep, too fresh to forget
The Berlin wall, a reminder of the bitter past for you
That through hate no one wins

All stand to lose
Wasted years not to relive
When friend was against friend
Family divided against family
To ideology to prostrate
At the expense of peace, progress, and prosperity.

Now overcomers you are!
Lessons learned, too good to be forgotten
To your land my sons and daughters come
Learning from your achievements
Discrimination not again to hear
That a world of peace we all may have
To our children and our children's children we may pass
And so, Germany we applaud you!

Italy, we applaud you!
Your years in Africa to reign
Now a hand of friendship you offer
That my sons and daughters
in harmony, they may with you live
from Somalia, they come
from Ethiopia, you receive them
And from Eritrea, refuge they find
A common destiny we now share
A different world we may live in
A peaceful world we may have!
And so, Italy we salute you!

Belgium, we applaud you!
For a change of heart, you now have!
A friend you have become!

Your past sins not to repeat
Your missionaries you had once ordered
That all natives of Belgium Congo
poor were to be
encouraged to give all they had to you!
For heaven was their share
Now friends and partners we are!
Yes, more than friends!

Now, "Belgian Aid to Africa" freely flows!
That to your friends you may give
Rendering help to the poor!
That your God now to bless
Wrongs rectified
Forgiveness and healing found
A mutual peace to find
And Belgium we salute you!

Scandinavians, we applaud you!
Your work among the poor is highly valued!
Unconditionally rendering help to the disadvantaged
As to the Lord, you serve
Sweden, a friend indeed,
Olof Palme, Africa still mourns you!
Died at the hands of an assassin
Because in justice you believed!
Sweden, Africa loves you!
Norway, an all-weather friend
Denmark, friendship unabridged!

The Netherlands we applaud you!
Injurious past to forget!

For we all grow out of our immaturity
Learning from our past mistakes
and making the best of the days
our bitter past not to remember
A contribution to South Africa,
a better Africa to have
Your destiny tied with us
That together we all may prosper
Our sons and daughters in your land to educate
Friendship developed
out of mutual respect for one another
And so, The Netherlands we applaud you!

The former Soviet Union we applaud you!
Russia, a friend to the oppressed!
Fighting for those with no voice
Arming the liberation struggle of mother Africa
To whom could Africa have turned but to you?
A cruel oppression to dismantle
Training my leaders to free her people
For no voice of reasoning or negotiation
could be heard or respected
Training my youth in agriculture, engineering, and
        medicine
that their people they may serve
And so, Russia we salute you!

We applaud you Russia!
Your birds you supplied
That we too may soar
The enemies' crafts to repel
That we too armed to the teeth we would be

An ally too important, too reliable to be forgotten!
For rough and hard times with you we endured
Granting education and training to thousands of Africans
in Russia!
And so, Russia we applaud you!

China, we remember!
We applaud you China!
Your aid unconditionally granted!
To Africa you freely gave
Building roads, rail lines, factories
Arming the freedom fighters!
For to the Left we had to turn
For the Right, then, not to help
A yoke so oppressive, too heavy to bear
A friend in China we found
A friend in Chairman Mao we found!
And so, China we applaud you!

Still no friend like you, China we see!
To your land, African students came
An education to obtain!
Physicians from your land freely you gave,
some of the best minds we had seen!
Your pledge to invest in Africa
Followed by action!
That Africa, like other developed continents,
she may be too!
No fear, of equipping the unequipped
A brother's keeper, ensuring that the left-behind may
        catch up too!
Massive investment and construction you bring,

and mutually we live together!
Both, to benefit from a mutual friendship!
China, O China! A friend indeed!

Cuba, O Cuba!
Loathed by many, a darling to Africa!
In sickness and in health
In need and in want
An all-weather friend to Africa you have been
Sacrificially giving and caring
Havana, we salute you!

Cuba, O Cuba!
We applaud you Cuba!
Angola remembers you!
Zambia pays homage
Namibia says, "Thank you!"
Mozambique deeply appreciates
Congo DR is grateful!
And South Africa ululates at you!
Cuba, O Cuba!
A darling of mother Africa you are!

My hospitals, your doctors freely you supply!
Free training my sons and daughters in your land you
        grant!
A helping hand to the needy and sick you give!
On the battlefront, your men you withhold not
To die with their brothers that freedom they may have
You ensured!
Land of Fidel Castro!
Cuba, O Cuba!

A darling of mother Africa you are!

"Yugoslavia," a friend to the oppressed!
"Yugoslavia," a divided nation you now are!
(Macedonia, Croatia, Serbia, Slovenia, Bosnia and
      Herzegovina).
we applaud you!
Land of Marshal Josip Broz Tito
Our armies you armed and dressed!
Your military training and aid to liberate a people
you provided!
"Yugo march" my army loves!
A cooperating partner in sport and in warfare!
African students to educate!
Federal Republic of Yugoslavia we applaud you!

Bulgaria, fellow comrades in the struggle
We applaud you!
Free scholarships to African youths you gave
With the downtrodden you identified yourselves!
Africa, your gifts never to forget!
And so, you too, Bulgaria we applaud!

Romania, land of Nicolae Ceausescu!
Romania, we applaud you!
Fellow comrades in the struggle!
Granting support to those who to the East
for help they looked!
Promoting agrarian revolution to the hungry
Support to the students of developing nations
you rendered!
Your sacrifice never to forget!

And so, Romania we applaud you!

Poland, our sons and daughters you educate!
Agricultural engineers, economists, and doctors to make
A friendship beyond ideology
Your sacrifice we applaud!
Doors opened for your partners in the struggle
That justice and equality we all may share
Poland, ye Poland we remember!

East Germany, our comrades!
There, our sons and daughters
To school they went
Admitted, prosperity to share
Meagre portions you had to give away
To share with others
For comrades, we were
Comrades we are!

A divided nation once you were
Pain felt, a common experience we share
Our continent divided too
Though, unknowingly, Berlin a part she played
Clan from clan taken away
Ethnic group from ethnic group
A divided Africa left to endure
A chasm too deep, too wide to bring together
And East Germany a friend in the struggle
A united Germany you now are!
Unity we all cherish to see and have
And so, Germany we applaud you!

CHAPTER 25
A CALL TO UNITY, A CALL TO VICTORY!

A call to unity, not to arms
A call to love, not to hate
A call to build, not to destroy
A call to dialogue, not to shun
A call to forgive, not to remember
A call to embrace, not to refrain
A call to heal, not to hurt
A call to peace, not to turmoil
A call to rest, not to distress
A call to reconcile, not to kill!

One Africa, one purpose, one goal
One continent, one people, one enemy
One currency, one passport, one national registration card
One leader, one government, one constitution
One parliament, one army, one nation
One voice, one stand, one revolution!

A time to empower, a time to reign
A time to overcome, a time to progress
A time to unify, a time to consolidate
A time to cease hostilities, a time to halt hatred
A time to come together, a time to build together

A time to work together, a time to live together!

For folly for us it would be
The present generation to be blamed
for the "sale" of their kin into slavery.
For folly it would be, the sins of the forefathers
to be heaped upon their children's children.

For folly for us it would be
to refuse to turn a blind eye at someone's wrongs
Wrongs that cannot be undone
For I heard someone say,
"An eye for an eye makes the whole world blind," [50]
    (Mahatma Gandhi).
Hence, a tooth for a tooth
makes the whole world toothless.
Forgiveness, the Master's command
"Love to cover over a multitude of sins," [51] (The Holy
    Bible, NIV James 5:20).

A time to forget and forgive
Someone's hatred not to remember
Slavery, a mistake of a people who had embraced it
Her descendants not to blame
For in all men wickedness is found
Colour, not an issue but man's heart
Africa, brotherhood of all men to embrace
A path to victory, the Master's desire.

A path to victory lies ahead
An open path to overcoming
It is a path of opportunity

Opportunity for all
It is a path that neither denies nor excludes
any man or woman
any child or adult
A path that is "colour-blind"
And knows no race, creed, religion or language
No name is a barrier to this path
And all who desire enter therein.

Victory is assured
Victory for Africa looms
When to blame others for our condition
we cease,
to point at someone else
for our present circumstances we stop,
when responsibility for our situation
we take.
A deliberate step to recognize
our poor state of affairs
To hide no longer in a perpetual maze of a blame game
and business.
Responsibility to take
To expound the unlimited power of the mind
that we possess
And its unlimited power to transcend all known barriers.

When our resources we choose wisely to use
Our ingenuity to harness
Our resources to good use to put
And our detractors and perpetrators of failure
to shame
That we too can achieve

We too can arise
For in man it is to overcome
In man, it is to prevail
Every hill and difficult to transcend and surmount
A rest for our sons and daughters to grant
That we too can achieve
This to them our promise to be:

We shall not agree with our circumstances
For our circumstances, we can change
Beyond the fault of those who have wronged us
we shall live
We shall not agree with the circumstances
we live in
And on no one else blame shall we heap on anymore
For the power to change our circumstances,
in us and in our hands, is.

Japan recognized, India acknowledged
And so, did China and South Korea
They all perceived and to change,
they determined
The power of words to destroy
Spoken words to a people
Injurious words meant to hurt
Jesus to heal
Hopelessness and failure to defeat
Forgiveness an antidote to heal the broken-hearted
And peace within to find
And in peace with others to live!

Africa! Power of agreement to pursue

Whining and complacence to stop
Like a phoenix, from ashes to arise!
Responsibility to accept
And victory and prosperity to have
And among the great Africa to be counted:

Africa, a success story in waiting
A positive work culture finally to embrace
Working hard for our children
An inheritance to give
Investments to have
A positive work culture to cultivate
Responsibility and integrity to share
Africa, a work ethics never to divorce
And high productivity to aim for
A new attitude to have
And good, high quality infrastructure, road
and rail network planning.

Government to enumerate its workers
with living wages
An equal work and equal pay for all
Industry not to discriminate
Hefty salaries and allowances for a different
colour group of workers
Peanuts for the locals
A long-time discrimination at workplace
from the colonial era to eradicate
Motivation for all workers to instil
And high productivity for Africa to have!

Collaborating with people who will help you

beat the system of institutionalized suffering and poverty
erected by the rich and strong
may be key to your development and emancipation
In China you now see that path
Mutual benefits to share
Their success story you too to learn
And Africa among the great soon to be!

New industries to harness
Policy of suppliers of raw materials for centuries
for all others to review
Our own manufacturing firms to make
For raw materials, enough we have
Our own sons and daughters, firms to own
companies and family businesses,
like our friends across the oceans.
Household names to maintain and build,
passed on from generation to generation.
Posterity not to fail to propagate family businesses
due to licentious and luxurious living
Sweat and ingenuity of founders not to throw to the dogs
And parents, their children, business principles to teach.
The widow's and her children's family wealth not to
        ransack
By hopeless and heartless extended family members
who desire to reap where they did not sow!

Cush, our roots to rediscover!
Our stolen identity to discover again!
The Creator's purpose for us, as a people to know again!

From the tribe of Benjamin, like Paul, we are! (Psalm 7;
　　Philippians 3:5, Acts 9:34; 21:37-39). [52] (The Holy
　　Bible, & all Scriptures below).
A stolen feat and unknown by your children!
A people sent to spread the good tidings of the death of
　　the Son of David, we are! (2 Samuel 18:21).
A people with an inheritance from Abraham (Keturah,
　　Genesis 25:1-6; 1 Chronicles 1:1-32-33).
Egypt, Sudan (Isaiah 18:1), Zimbabwe, Persia, Ethiopia
　　and Libya (Ezekiel 38:5-7) with our heads high to
　　walk!
Shame, a bygone word among you must be!
Sheba, son of Jokshan son of Abraham
The kingdom of Sheba, whose queen visited Solomon,
　　(1 King 10:1-13; 2 Chronicles 9:1-12), to recall!
Ethiopia, my roots to embrace again, (Acts 8:26-40).
Moses, his wife Zipporah (Daughter of Jethro, also
　　called Reuel, a Cushite) not to forget! (Exodus
　　2:19-25; 4:18-26; 18:1-6; Numbers 12:1-16.)
Cush, not an afterthought in God's plan!
Africa, my Africa!

Jealous for one another to throw away!
A friend's success all to be proud of
As our success story, too
A rising friend never to pull down
Others to teach that they too may succeed
Burdens to share, burdens lifted
A threat in your neighbour not to see
Like the way in the village we lived
A common ancestry we have
A brother's keeper once again to be

And Africa, mother Africa
A continent of pride and a "nation" to be proud of
A great nation and a great people
And forever to cherish!
Africa, mother Africa!

"Envy thou not the oppressor, and choose none of his ways," Proverbs 3:31 (KJV).

Song: Give a Thought to Africa, John Knox Bokwe (1855-1922)

1. Give a thought to Africa! 'neath the burning Sun
   There are hosts of weary hearts, waiting to be won
   Many lives have passed away; and in many homes
   There are voices crying now, to the living God.

Chorus:

   Tell the love of Jesus
   By the hills and waters
   God bless Africa,
   And her sons and daughters

2. Give your love to Africa! They are brothers all
   Who by sin and slavery, long were held in thrall
   Let the white man love the black; and, when time is
       past
   In our Father's home above all shall meet at last.

3. Give support to Africa! Has not British gold
   Been the gain of tears and blood, when the slaves
       were sold?
   Let us send the Gospel back, since for all their need
   Those whom Jesus Christ makes free, shall be free
       indeed.

Africa, Mayo Africa (Bemba – Zambia) Africa, My Africa, Mpundu Mutale,
(September 30, 1935 – August 1, 2006)

1. *"Africa, mayo Africa," Ba mama baleimba*
   Mululamba lwa chimana, nshatala nkumona
   Namona 'mulopa obe uwaitike pamushili obe
   Umulopa walibe lyobe, ilibe lya kucula kobe
   Africa, mayo Africa.

2. *Africa, njeba Africa, Ukucula kwa busha bobe*
   Ubusha bwabana bobe, Bushe uleya kunuma?
   Naumfwe 'shiwi aliti, "Uwaculile mukulwisha kobe."
   Umulopa walibe lyobe, ilibe lya kucula kobe
   Africa, mayo Africa.

Narration

   "Bushe Africa obe?" Naine nati, "Ee, e mayo!"
   Ndetotela abo bonse abapwishishe ubusha
   Nokuleta umutende mucalo ca Africa
   Ubulwi, ukucimfya, ne mfwa. Ukwibukisha inshiku
       shapita
   Umulopa walibe lyobe, ilibe lya kucula kobe
   Africa, mayo Africa.

3. *"Africa, mayo Africa," Ba mama baleimba*
   Mululamba lwa chimana, nshatala nkumona
   Namona 'mulopa obe uwaitike pamushili obe
   Umulopa walibe lyobe, ilibe lya kucula kobe
   Africa, mayo Africa.

1. "Africa, my Africa," my grandmother singing
   Beside a distant river, I have never seen you before
   By my gaze full of your blood, your blood-flood
       spilled over the field
   The blood of your sweat, the sweat of your toil
   Africa, my Africa.

2. Africa, tell me Africa, the toil of your slavery
   The slavery of your children, 're you going back to
       that pain?
   Solemnly a voice answers me, "You've tasted a bitter
       taste of liberty."
   The blood of your sweat, the sweat of your toil
   Africa, my Africa.

Narration

   "Is Africa, your Africa?" I answer, "Yes, is my mother!"
   And I praise the men who sought to end slave trade
   And bring peace to Africa's land, the fight, the victory,
       the death
   The memories of bygone days, the blood of your
       sweat, the sweat of your toil
   Africa, my Africa.

3. "Africa, my Africa," my grandmother singing
   Beside a distant river, I have never seen you before
   By my gaze full of your blood, your blood-flood
       spilled over the field
   The blood of your sweat, the sweat of your toil
   Africa, my Africa!⁵³

Zambian National Anthem
[Tune from Nkosi Sikelel'i Africa, (God bless Africa)
    Enoch Sontonga 1897, Methodist School Teacher]

1. Stand and sing of Zambia, proud and free
    Land of work and joy in unity,
    Victors in the struggle for the right,
    We have won freedom's fight
    All one, strong and free.

2. Africa is our own mother land
    Fashion'd with and blessed by God's good hand,
    Let us all her people join as one,
    Brothers under the sun.
    All one, strong and free.

3. One land and one nation is our cry,
    Dignity and peace 'neath Zambia's sky,
    Like our noble eagle in its flight,
    Zambia, praise to thee.
    All one, strong and free.

Chorus:

    Praise be to God,
    Praise be, praise be, praise be,
    Bless our great nation,
    Zambia, Zambia, Zambia.
    Free men we stand
    Under the flag of our land.
    Zambia, praise to thee!
    All one, strong and free.

Charles Kapungwe

African Union Anthem

1. Let us all unite and celebrate together
   The victories won for our liberation
   Let us dedicate ourselves to rise together
   To defend our liberty and unity.

O Sons and Daughters of Africa
Flesh of the Sun and Flesh of the Sky
Let us make Africa the Tree of Life.

2. Let us all unite and sing together
   To uphold the bonds that frame our destiny
   Let us dedicate ourselves to fight together
   For lasting peace and justice on earth.

O Sons and Daughters of Africa
Flesh of the Sun and Flesh of the Sky
Let us make Africa the Tree of Life.

3. Let us all unite and toil together
   To give the best we have to Africa
   The cradle of mankind and fount of culture
   Our pride and hope at break of dawn.

O Sons and Daughters of Africa
Flesh of the Sun and Flesh of the Sky
Let us make Africa the Tree of Life.

Rev. Dr. Paul Bupe and Rev. Charles Kapungwe with Zambia's first Republic leader, President Kenneth David Kaunda at Clarion Town House Hotel in Columbia, South Carolina, U.S.A. 18 March, 2003.

Mr. Finnbar Dunphy, a former resident of Zambia, Zambia's first Republic leader, President Kenneth David Kaunda and Rev. Charles Kapungwe at South Trust Building in Columbia, South Carolina, U.S.A. 20 March, 2003.

Bibliography

1. Ali Alamin Mazrui. *The Africans: A triple heritage,* 1986
2. The Declaration of Independence. ushistory.org July, 1995 retrieved on August 5, 2011 from http://www. ushistory.org/declaration/document/
3. *The Holy Bible*, NIV ® Copyright © 1973, 1978, 1984 by International Bible Society
4. Julie Rose. NPR, June 22, 2011. N.C. Considers Paying Forced Sterilization Victims. Retrieved on April 21, 2012 from http://www.npr.org/2011/06/22/137347548/n-c-considers-paying-forced-sterilization-victims
5. *The Holy Bible*, NIV ® Copyright © 1973, 1978, 1984 by International Bible Society
6. Citation could not be found News media – under Laurent Kabila's Presidency.
7. Mark Doyle BBC News Africa, Retrieved 21 June, 2012 from http://www.bbc.co.uk/news/world-africa-18538997
8. *The Holy Bible*, NIV ® Copyright © 1973, 1978, 1984 by International Bible Society
9. Orwell, George. *Animal Farm*, 1945
10. Martin Luther King Jr. I have a dream, 1963. Retrieved on August 5, 2011 from http://juntosociety.com/hist_speeches/mlkihad.html
11. CIA releases files on past misdeeds. The Washington Post, June 27, 2007 retrieved on August 5, 2011 from http://www.washingtonpost.com/wp-dyn/content/article/2007/06/26/AR2007062600861.html
12. Anonymous
13. Haley, Alex. *The Autobiography of Malcolm X* as told to Alex Haley, 1965

14. *The Holy Bible*, NIV ® Copyright © 1973, 1978, 1984 by International Bible Society. Matthew 2:15 NIV, 1984

15. *The Holy Bible*, KJV Psalm 24:1 KJV, 1979

16. Chitonga, Jameson. Personal communication, 1979

17. Kaunda, Joe. *The Post*. Zambia: Emily castigates Anglo over KCM pull out. Sikazwe, Emily. The wheels of capitalism are driven by blood, February 11, 2002 retrieved on August 19, 2011 from http://allafrica.com/stories/200202110503.html

18. Mwanawasa, Levy P. Anglo American plc. $30m environmental bill for Anglo American to quit Zambian mine retrieved on August 8, 2011 from http://www.knowmore.org/wiki/index.php?title=Anglo_American_plc June 2002

19. Field, L. (2019, February 5). What Happened to All the Black Farmers? Retrieved October 24, 2019, from https://www.youtube.com/watch?v=q-VWIZIL4ag

20. Burns, R. (2019, October 15). Trump threatens to 'destroy' Turkey's economy with sanctions. Retrieved October 21, 2019, from https://news.yahoo.com/trump-imposes-sanctions-turkey-threatens-040656249.html

21. Mumba, Nevers. *Israel Had No Weapons*

22. The Holy Bible, NIV ® Copyright © 1973, 1978, 1984 by International Bible Society. Ecclesiastes 9:11

23. Patrick Bond, Cultivating African Anti-Capitalism, April 2005 retrieved on August 8, 2011 from http://www.bnvillage.co.uk/village-square/77264-cultivating-african-anti-capitalism-patrick-bond.html

24. Patrick Bond, Cultivating African Anti-Capitalism, April 2003. Third World Traveller. *Z Magazine*. February 2003. Accessed January 31, 2015 from http://www.thirdworldtraveler.com/Africa/African_Anticapitalism.html

25. Wurmbrand, Richard. Tortured for Christ, 1964

26. Sarafina – Leleti Khumalo, Whoopi Goldberg, 1992

27. Memorable quotes by Martin Luther King Jr. Sixteenth Street Baptist Church, Birmingham, Alabama, May 3, 1963 retrieved on August 23, 2011 from http://www.africawithin.com/mlking/king_quotes.htm

28. Washington State University. Famous quotes. Martin Luther King Jr. Don't allow anybody to make you feel that you're nobody. Always feel that you count, 1967 retrieved on August 23, 2011 from http://mlk.wsu.edu/default.asp?PageID=1481

29. Martin Kaponde. Britain abandons vulture fund. *Zambia Daily Mail*, June 29, 2010

30. President George Bush. Africa is out of the picture

31. Winsor, M. (2019, October 21). Congo's Ebola outbreak, now concentrated in a gold mining area, remains a global emergency: WHO. Retrieved October 25, 2019, from https://abcnews.go.com/International/congos-ebola-outbreak-now-concentrated-gold-mining-area/story?id=66415616

32. *Congo Stories: Battling Five Centuries of Exploitation and Greed*. Prendergast, John & Bafilemba, Fidel. Hachette Book Group, 1290 Avenue of the Americas, New York NY.

33. Stockwell, John. October 1987. The secret wars of the CIA retrieved on August 9, 2011 from http://www.informationclearinghouse.info/article4068.htm

34. Martin Luther King Jr. Now is the time to make democracy a reality

35. AF Acronym Finder. BOMA British Overseas Management Administration retrieved on August 19, 2011 from http://www.acronymfinder.com/British-Overseas-Management-Administration-(BOMA).html

36. *The Elders.* Nelson Mandela biography retrieved on August 23, 2011 from http://www.theelders.org/elders/nelson-mandela

37. A preacher in Columbia, South Carolina

38. *Stone of Hope,* Columbia SC. Martin Luther King Jr. Remaining awake through a great revolution. National Cathedral (Episcopal), Washington, DC March 31, 1968 retrieved on August 23, 2011 from http://www.waymarking.com/waymarks/WM9FF8_Stone_of_Hope_Columbia_SC

39. *Stone of Hope,* Columbia, SC. Martin Luther King Jr. I have been to the mountain top, Memphis, Tennessee, April 3, 1968 retrieved on August 23, 2011 from http://www.waymarking.com/waymarks/WM9FF8_Stone_of_Hope_Columbia_SC

40. *Stone of Hope,* Columbia, SC. Martin Luther King Jr. Injustice anywhere is a threat to justice everywhere, Letter from Birmingham City Jail, Birmingham, Alabama, April 16, 1965 retrieved on August 23, 2011 from http://www.waymarking.com/waymarks/WM9FF8_Stone_of_Hope_Columbia_SC.

41. President Kenneth Kaunda personal communication, 2003

42. *The Holy Bible,* NIV ® Copyright © 1973, 1978, 1984 by International Bible Society. Proverbs 24:6

43. *The Holy Bible* Proverbs 11:14 KJV, 1979

44. *NIV Study Bible.* Matthew 26:52; John 18:11

45. *NIV Study Bible* Matthew 5:43-44, Romans 12:20.

46. Zenovia, B. Kanye West's big mouth gets him in trouble again, November 26, 2006 retrieved on August 15, 2011 from http://www.associatedcontent.com/article/92845/kanye_wests_big_mouth_gets_him_in_trouble.html?cat=38

47. Joseph Grant Swank, March, 2005. God speaks through earthquakes retrieved on August 10, 2011 from http://www.paklinks.com/gs/religion-and-scripture/178629-god-speaks-through-earthquakes.html

48. Thomas Jefferson Quotes®.net, August 2011 retrieved on August 15, 2011 from http://www.quotes.net/quote/8098

49. U.S. constitution online. Martin Luther King Jr. I have a dream, 1963 retrieved on August 23, 2011 from http://www.usconstitution.net/dream.html

50. Gandhi, Mahatma. Infoplease. Mohandas Gandhi, ©2000-2011 Pearson Education retrieved on August 24, 2011 from http://www.infoplease.com/biography/var/mohandasgandhi.html

51. *The Holy Bible*, NIV ® Copyright © 1973, 1978, 1984 by International Bible Society. James 5:20

52. *The Holy Bible*, NIV.

53. Marvin Mulenga: https://www.youtube.com/watch?v=WtBK4PLF6zw Retrieved on February 6, 2018. (Lyrics written based on listening to audio recording)

FOR FURTHER READING AND WATCHING

Jake Rudnitsky & Evgenia Pismennaya. Oil plunge magnifies Russia's sanctions pain: Chart of the day. Bloomberg. October 7, 2014. http://www.bloomberg.com/news/2014-10-07/oil-plunge-magnifies-russia-s-sanctions-pain-chart-of-the-day.html

Peggy McIntosh. White privilege: unpacking the invisible knapsack. (Excerpted essay is printed from Winter 1990 issue of *Independent School*). http://ted.coe.wayne.edu/ele3600/mcintosh.html

Tim Wise. Breaking the cycle of white dependence: A modest call for majority self-help. (Published as a ZNet Commentary). *TimeWise*. May 19, 2001. http://www.timwise.org/2001/05/breaking-the-cycle-of-white-dependence-a-modest-call-for-majority-self-help/

Harriet A. Washington. *Medical Apartheid: The Dark History of Medical Experimentation on Black Americans from Colonial Times to the Present*. Krause, Kai. The true size of Africa. 2015. Retrieved on August 18, 2015 from http://kai.sub.blue/en/africa.html

Derek Luke, Tim Robbins. *Catch A Fire*. 2007. Universal Studios. 10 Universal City Plaza, Universal City CA 91608

CBS NEWS. *60 Minutes*. A lying undercover agent arrested 46 people, most of them black, on drug charges. (June 21, 2020). Tulia, Texas. Accessed August 16, 2020. http://cbsn.ws/1Qkjo1F [One of the worst miscarriages of justice in U.S. history. Tom Coleman an undercover agent hired by a local Sheriff in 1998 to get rid of "drug dealers" (or Blacks to put it truthfully) who were sent to prison for a total of 750 years!] WATCH!! Money used to hire Coleman came from the U.S. Department of Justice (or to put it rightly, U.S. Department of Injustice). Arrested 13% of Tulia's adult Black population in 1999 by one person!

INDEX